How to Forgive

John Monbourquette

How to Forgive

A Step-by-Step Guide

NOVALIS

ST. ANTHONY MESSENGER PRESS

Cincinnati, Ohio

DARTON·LONGMAN+TODD

© 2000 Novalis, Saint Paul University, Ottawa, Canada

Cover: Blair Turner
Layout: Blaine Herrmann and Blair Turner

Translators: Kathy Poor and Bernadette Gasslein
Editor: Bernadette Gasslein

Business Office:
Novalis
49 Front Street East, 2nd Floor
Toronto, Ontario, Canada M5E 1B3

Phone: 1-800-387-7164 or (416) 363-3303
Fax: 1-800-204-4140 or (416) 363-9409
E-mail: novalis@interlog.com

First published in French in 1992 by Novalis and les Éditions du Centurion.
English translation published in 2000 by Novalis, Saint Paul University, Ottawa, Canada
        and Darton, Longman and Todd Ltd, 1 Spencer Court,
        140-142 Wandsworth High Street, London SW18 4JJ U.K.
        Published and distributed in the United States of America by
        St. Anthony Messenger Press
        1615 Republic St.
        Cincinnati, OH 45210
        1-800-488-0488
        www.AmericanCatholic.org

We acknowledge the financial support of the Government of Canada through the Book Publishing Industry Development Program (BPIDP) for our publishing activities.

Canadian Cataloguing in Publication Data

Monbourquette, Jean
    How to forgive: a step-by-step guide
Translation of Comment Pardonner?
Includes bibliographical references
ISBN 2-89507-022-9

    1. Forgiveness. I. Title.

BJ1476.M6513 2000   179'.9   00-900634-6

A catalogue record for this book is available from the British Library.

ISBN 0-232-52391-6

ISBN (U.S.) 0-86716-427-1
Printed in Canada

About the author

John Monbourquette is a psychotherapist, bestselling author and Roman Catholic priest. While he has both taught high school and worked as a parish priest, his principal interest has been in the relationship between spirituality and psychology. His graduate studies in theology and psychology, and his doctoral studies in psychology at the International College of Los Angeles, have enabled him to pursue these interests both in the academic world, where he is a professor in the Institut de Pastorale of Saint Paul University, Ottawa, and in his own private practice as a psychologist. His special areas of interest include forgiveness, self-esteem, male violence, the dynamics of grief, and accompanying the dying.

He has given hundreds of conferences on these topics in Canada and Europe to both professional and lay audiences. He is the author (under his French name, Jean Monbourquette) of eight books in French, one of which has sold over 150,000 copies. Two of these (*To Love Again* and *Growing Through Loss*) have already been translated into English; a third, *Befriending Your Shadow*, will be available in 2001. He is co-author of three other books and has written many articles for professional journals.

*I dedicate this book to Jacques Croteau,
my friend and mentor*

TABLE OF CONTENTS

What does it take to forgive? This question has intrigued me for the better part of ten years. I have found myself forced to come to terms with the difficulty of forgiving, even as I have found my readers, clients, and those I have helped guide along their spiritual journey struggling with the same problem.

This book is the result of a great deal of research and reflection, along with my clinical work with clients and my own psychological and spiritual awareness. My intention in writing is clear: to provide a practical guide that can teach you to forgive if you follow its steps.

Several people have asked me: "Why twelve steps? That seems like a lot!" I agree. But, as you may suspect, I didn't just hit on that idea all at once. Rather, it came to me after I noticed how some people, no matter how much they wanted to forgive, felt stymied at certain points along the way. As I worked at untangling their confusion, I became aware of the complexity of the psychological and spiritual dynamics of forgiving. With every new insight and every new difficulty, I ended up adding another step.

How should you use this book? The most important thing is to respect your own ways of doing things and your own manner of forgiving. Some of you will read this book from cover to cover. Others will prefer to concentrate on a particular teaching, depending on your needs at the time. Some chapters will seem very familiar, while others will appear new and unexplored. If you find a particular chapter especially relevant, take the time to study it in more depth and carry out the exercises it suggests. Gradually, you will be more in tune with your own emotional states, more aware of your blockages; you will find ways to resolve these and move on successfully. To each of you, I say: "Enjoy this inner journey in search of the forgiveness that will allow you to heal and grow!"

While you will find here many stories inspired by the Christian tradition, *How to Forgive* is written for the largest possible number of readers, whether you profess religious faith or not. Some of you may not be comfortable using "God" in describing the spiritual aspects of forgiveness. Feel free to use a term that better suits your own spiritual orientation, such as "Transcendent," "Higher Self," "Divine Source or Energy," or "Unconditional Love."

As I reach the end of this Foreword, I want to thank my fellow Oblate priest, Jacques Croteau, for his encouragement and unfailing interest in the completion of my work. He reviewed the original French manuscript to make sure that it was absolutely clear.

PART ONE

Exploring the Nature of Forgiveness

"What are you trying to learn about yourself by writing a book on forgiveness?" This question, put to me by a friend whom I had told about my project, took me aback and made me think. Until that point, I had thought that the needs of others were motivating my decision to write about forgiveness. Upon reflection, however, I realized that I had undertaken this project mainly for myself. For more than three years, I had been struggling to recover from a hurt. I had thought that all my bitterness would be miraculously dispelled through a purely deliberate act of forgiveness. It did not work. I could not find that dearly sought-after inner peace.

This realization was one of the main events that led me to my study of the dynamics of forgiveness. I asked myself why, despite all my best intentions and repeated efforts, I was unable to break free of my resentment. I had the feeling that I was wasting my time and energy by uselessly rehashing the past.

The more I tried to forgive, the less I succeeded. I felt afraid, guilty and angry. Sometimes, in the midst of this inner chaos, I would experience a few short-lived bursts of mercy and fleeting moments of inner release. At other times, I became hopeful that I would finally be able to overcome my desire for revenge, but this feeling would quickly be replaced by sudden flares of aggression and wounded pride. That was when I understood that, despite my long years of religious, philosophical, theological and pastoral training, I was a mere beginner in the art of forgiving. So, I started to read up on the subject and to examine my own experiences and those of

my students and clients. I wanted to discover once and for all
what was blocking my efforts at forgiveness. Could I ever
hope to see light at the end of the tunnel?

One event became the determining factor. I witnessed a
psychological and physical healing that resulted from an exercise in forgiving. I was treating a 55-year-old man in psychotherapy – a deeply religious university professor. His
immersion in his work and his family problems had led him
to the verge of depression and to stomach ulcers. It only took
about ten sessions for my client to learn to release his suffering
by expressing, in the most literal sense of the word, his disappointment with and his frustration and anger at his wife for
her addiction to alcohol, at his son for his drug habit and at
his daughter for her infatuation with a young man he could
not stand. This progressive release, based on an acceptance of
what he perceived as negative feelings, brought him profound
relief. During one therapy session, when I was feeling somewhat short of ideas, I decided to use the empty chair, or
rather chairs, technique, where each chair represents a family
member. I then suggested that he forgive each one. It was a
very moving encounter. My client often found himself in
tears while he expressed his forgiveness. And then, without
any prompting from me, he spontaneously turned to each of
them and asked their forgiveness for his frequent absences and
lack of interest. Two weeks after this session, he announced
that his ulcers had healed. I was at a loss to explain how forgiveness could heal physical ailments.

Readers of my book *To Love Again* (Novalis, 1993) often
write to tell me that they run into trouble while reading the
pages on forgiveness. They all agree that forgiveness is beautiful and necessary, but they wonder how to get to that point. I

can't tell you how many people I have met who, like these readers, despair of ever being able to forgive. They feel like they are walking towards a star that keeps retreating as they get closer.

Such a feeling of powerlessness is often increased when we hear about examples of forgiveness that tend to be easier to admire than to imitate. How could anyone even think of imitating Pope John Paul II as he forgave the man who tried to assassinate him, or Gandhi as he taught non-violence and forgiveness towards his persecutors, let alone Jesus as he implored God to forgive his tormentors even as he hung on the cross? We feel we can't measure up to such giants of forgiveness. It's a bit like being sent out to catch a whale with nothing but a little fishing rod.

Few psycho-spiritual realities have been as misunderstood or misrepresented as forgiveness. And yet, forgiveness holds a central place in the spirituality of the major religions, in particular, Christianity. I do not claim that my reflections represent the final word on the subject of forgiveness. What I propose is more modest. First, I break down a few commonly held misconceptions about forgiveness. We tend to overuse the term and simplify it to the point of ridicule. We use it as a catch-all for realities that have nothing to do with it, thereby leading too many people who are in a hurry to forgive into psychological and spiritual impasses. Then, I present theories on the nature of forgiveness to help you both to avoid the pitfalls of false notions of forgiveness and to understand the true nature of the act.

In the second part, I propose a way of learning to forgive based on a twelve-step process. Practical applications follow each step. I am convinced that this journey will bring wounded hearts to find the peace and inner freedom they so fervently long for.

17

As Life Is Renewed

Must winter forgive spring,
and spring, summer?
Must summer forgive autumn,
and autumn, winter?
Must night forgive day;
and the sun, the moon?
Must lovers forgive each other
for yearning both to be together
and to be free?
Must a mother forgive her newborn;
a father, his independent and rebellious child?
Must the child in each of us
forgive the adolescent;
the adolescent, the adult;
the adult, the elder?
Must we forgive God
his imperfect creation?
Must God forgive us
for wanting to resemble him?

CHAPTER I

The Importance of Forgiveness in Our Lives

Do you want to be happy for a moment? Then seek revenge.
Do you want to be happy forever? Then grant forgiveness.

—HENRI LACORDAIRE

At some point, each of us needs to forgive in order to re-establish peace and continue living with one another.

[handwritten margin note:] Dr Phil "Trust yourself" "have the ability to handle the problem if someone fails you."

There will always be a place for forgiveness in our lives. To recognize the burning need for it, spend just a bit of time listening to people pour out their hearts. No one escapes the pain of frustration, disappointment, betrayal, problems, or conflicts in love. Evidence of the hardships of living together abounds: conflicts between couples, within families, between separated lovers or divorced people, between bosses and employees, between friends or neighbours, among races or nations. At some point, each of us needs to forgive in order to re-establish peace and continue living with one another. When I asked a couple who were celebrating their fiftieth wedding anniversary for the secret of their lasting happiness, the wife replied: "Never once, after quarrelling, did we go to sleep without asking each other for forgiveness."

To discover the full importance of forgiveness, we should try to imagine what a world without forgiveness would be like. What would be the consequences? We would be condemned to choose among these four possibilities: perpetuate the grief suffered within ourselves and in others; live with resentment; remain fixated on the past; or seek revenge. Let us examine these options more closely.

PERPETUATING THE GRIEF
When our physical, moral or spiritual integrity has been hurt, something significant happens inside us. A part of our being

19

Imitating our aggressor is a well-known defence mechanism.

feels assaulted, bruised – I would even say sullied and violated – as if the offender's maliciousness had touched the most intimate parts of our being. We tend to mimic our offender, as if we had somehow been contaminated by a contagious virus. As a result of this mimicking, which tends to be more or less conscious, we are in turn inclined to be mean, not only towards the offender, but also towards ourselves and others. A man told me of the difficulties he was finding in living with a recently divorced woman: "Sometimes I feel as if she's making me pay for her ex-husband's stupidity."

Imitating our aggressor is a well-known defence mechanism. In what amounts to survival instinct, the victim identifies with the torturer. The magnificent Danish film *Pélé the Conqueror* portrays this. We are at pains to understand how a child as gentle as Pélé can so enjoy beating his mentally handicapped buddy. It all becomes clear, however, when we remember that Pélé is only replaying with an innocent victim the behaviour of the farm boy who had so humiliated him by whipping him. The same phenomenon appears in the epic film *Lawrence of Arabia*. We witness a radical change in the character of the hero, who, after he is tortured, becomes a completely different human being. He goes from being peaceful and kind-hearted to being sadistically aggressive. How many sexual aggressors and violent abusers do nothing but repeat the injuries perpetrated on them in their youth? In family therapy we often see that, in stressful situations, children adopt behaviour which mimics that of their parents. On the international scene, we come face to face with nations that employ against other peoples the same inhumane measures they once endured.

Here I am not speaking of vengeance as such, but of the reflexes buried in the individual or collective subconscious. This

Only forgiveness can break the chain reaction.

is why in forgiveness, we do not merely settle for not seeking revenge. Instead, we must go right to the root of all deviant, aggressive tendencies to eradicate them from our very being and stop their devastating effects before it is too late. Any predisposition to hostility and to domination of others risks being transmitted from generation to generation through families and cultures. Only forgiveness can break the chain reaction and stop these repeated gestures of vengeance, transforming them into gestures that bring life.

LIVING WITH CONSTANT RESENTMENT

Many people suffer from living with constant resentment. Let's take, for example, divorced people. Recent studies on the long-term effects of divorce have shown that many divorced people, especially women, continue to harbour a great deal of resentment towards their ex-spouse, sometimes even after fifteen years of separation. In my clinical experience, I have often noted that certain extreme emotional reactions result from the re-opening of an old wound that had healed poorly.

Yet, living in anger, even subconsciously, eats up a great deal of energy and maintains constant stress. We can better understand what happens if we keep in mind the difference between resentment, which produces stress, and anger, which does not. Resentment is a form of disguised anger that festers around a badly healed wound. Anger is a healthy emotion that disappears once it has been expressed; resentment and hostility settle in as defensive attitudes that are always ready to respond to real or imagined onslaughts. In this way, those who were dominated and humiliated in childhood are determined to never again allow themselves to be mistreated. To prevent mistreatment, they must constantly remain on guard. What is more, they are

21

People who will not or cannot forgive have trouble living in the now.

inclined to invent stories of conspiracies or attacks against them. Only the in-depth healing born of forgiveness can relieve this inner tension.

Resentment has other detrimental effects. It is at the origin of several psychosomatic illnesses. Stress created by resentment eventually attacks the immune system. Because the latter is constantly in a state of alert, it does not know how to identify the enemy. It no longer recognizes disease-causing agents. It can even attack healthy organs that it is supposed to defend. Herein lies the explanation for the origin of several illnesses such as arthritis, arteriosclerosis, multiple sclerosis, cardiovascular diseases, and diabetes. Dr. W. Redford (1989: 42) recommends the systematic practice of forgiveness in our daily lives as one of the best defense strategies against the detrimental effects of resentment.

After describing the various scientific studies on the links between negative emotional states and the appearance of cancer, Dr. Carl Simonton dedicates an entire chapter in his book *Getting Well Again* (New York: Bantam Books, 1992) to demonstrating that forgiveness remains the best way to overcome the devastation of resentment. With the help of mental imagery techniques, he invites people who suffer from cancer to project good wishes upon those who have hurt them. Those who have used his technique have detected a notable reduction in their stress levels and have felt better equipped to fight their illness. It is nothing short of amazing that such a simple approach to forgiveness could have such beneficial results.

STAYING MIRED IN THE PAST

People who will not or cannot forgive have trouble living in the now. They cling to the past and, in so doing, condemn them-

In the dynamics of bereavement, forgiveness represents a major and decisive step.

selves both to miss out on the present and to block off the future. In Eugene O'Neill's play *A Long Day's Journey into Night,* Mary Tyrone wears herself out by constantly rehashing a past that is both painful and closed to forgiveness. She becomes a burden and annoyance to her family. Her exasperated husband begs her: "Mary, for the love of God, forget the past!" To which she replies: "Why? How could I? The past is the present, is it not? And it is also the future. We all try to deny it, but life just won't let us." Her powerlessness to forgive has paralyzed her life. Memories of the past return to increase her old pain. She fritters away the here and now in useless reflection; time goes by, but she feels no happiness; any possibility of finding joy in human relationships is erased. The future is blocked and menacing: she creates no new emotional links, undertakes no new projects, embraces no stimulating risks. Life is anchored in the past.

My clinical experience with those mourning the death of or separation from loved ones has shown to me that forgiveness is the benchmark by which we determine whether full detachment from the loved one has occurred. Once I can get a person to admit their hurt, clean up their emotional universe and discover the meaning of their hurt, I invite that person to do one session of forgiveness: forgiveness of self, to eliminate all inner traces of guilt, and forgiveness of the loved one who is gone, to expel all remnants of resentment brought on by the separation. In the dynamics of bereavement, forgiveness represents a major and decisive step. It prepares the soul for the next step, that of "remembering," in which the person in mourning recovers all that he or she loved in the other. Later on, I will describe this re-membering phase in greater detail, as well as the ritual that can enable someone to enter into it (see Chapter 19).

The instinct for revenge blinds anyone who gives in to it.

SEEKING REVENGE

The after-effects of a life without forgiveness offer nothing satisfying, as we have just seen. Is revenge more fulfilling? Without a doubt it is a more instinctive and more spontaneous response to an offence. Yet, writes J.M. Pohier (1977: 233), trying to compensate for our own suffering by inflicting it on the offender gives to suffering magical powers that it does not possess. No doubt, picturing the offender humiliated and suffering produces a kind of narcissistic joy in whoever seeks vengeance. It spreads a temporary balm over their own suffering and humiliation. It lets the injured party feel that they are no longer alone in their misery. But at what price? It is nothing but fleeting satisfaction that lacks real fulfillment and relational creativity.

Revenge is a form of instinctive justice that emerges from the primitive gods of the unconscious. It seeks to re-establish equality based on the mutual inflicting of suffering. In the Jewish tradition, the famous *lex talionis*, which demanded "An eye for an eye, a tooth for a tooth," was intended to regulate revenge. It sought to soften the words of Lamech, son of Cain, who said to his wives: "I kill a man for wounding me, a young man for a blow. If sevenfold vengeance was to be exacted for Cain, for Lamech it would be seventy-sevenfold" (Genesis 4. 23-24). The instinct for revenge blinds anyone who gives in to it. How can someone determine precisely the exact amount of their suffering in order to exact equivalent suffering from the perpetrator? In truth, the offender and the victim get involved in an endlessly escalating exchange in which it becomes more and more difficult to judge that the blows are equivalent. Think of the classic example of the Mafia vendettas where killings of innocent people continue from one generation to the next.

Forgiveness alone can break the infernal cycle of vengeance and create new modes of human relationships.

Certainly, in everyday life, vendettas are less bloody. They are nonetheless extremely harmful to human relationships.

Seeking to "give as good as you get" to an offender throws both the victim and the perpetrator into a repetitive pattern. In the dance of revenge, we are more follower than leader, following the lead of the perpetrator only to find ourselves dragged into responding with equally vile actions. Obsession with revenge locks us into a spiral of violence. Forgiveness alone can break the infernal cycle of vengeance and create new modes of human relationships.

When a climate of revenge sets in, we often forget its destructive impact on our whole milieu. In one educational institution, a personality conflict between a principal and a teacher degenerated to the point where battle lines were drawn between two factions of the teaching staff. The climate of mistrust and suspicion spread to the students. The working and learning environments became more and more oppressive and painful. Such a situation shows the prime importance of an attitude of forgiveness in people in positions of authority. If they allow themselves to be led by a spirit of vindictiveness, we can expect conflicts to reach enormous and uncontrollable proportions among their staff.

The satisfaction that revenge provides is short-lived. It cannot compensate for the damage it produces in the network of human relations. Furthermore, revenge triggers cycles of violence that are hard to break. An obsession with revenge contributes nothing to healing the victim's wounds, but instead makes them worse. Still, while we should not think that in itself the decision to forgive constitutes forgiveness, it is the first important and decisive step on the road to forgiveness.

CHAPTER 2

A Tale of Forgiveness: Al and Adele

No one can ✔
change the past,
but you have the
power, as of this
moment, to see it
differently.

On the outskirts of a quiet village housing a few small businesses and shops stands a farm with freshly painted buildings. Surrounded by fields of various hues marked off by nice straight furrows is the farm belonging to Al, a proud, honest man of few words. Tall, slim, with a pointed chin and aquiline nose, he is as much feared as respected by the locals. He is not very talkative, but when he speaks, proverbs on the value of work or the meaning of life fall from his lips.

Adele, his wife, always has a warm smile and welcoming words. People feel good in her presence. This woman is all round: her face, her bosom, her hips.

Adele suffers silently, enduring a husband who is miserly both with words and caresses. Deep down, she regrets having married this "hard-working man" whom her now-deceased father so admired. Certainly, Al provides well for her and is faithful, but his total absorption in his work leaves little time for intimacy and pleasure.

One day, instead of working until dusk, Al comes home early. To his great dismay, he finds Adele in bed with a neighbour. The man flees through the window, while Adele, distraught, throws herself at Al's feet to beg his forgiveness. He remains as unmoved as a statue: face white with indignation, lips blue with rage, he barely manages to contain the flood of emotions that assault him. As he faces this betrayal, his feelings range from humiliation through deep pain to anger. Man of few words that he is, he cannot think of a thing to say. Soon he realizes, however, that the silent treatment he is inflicting on Adele tortures her far more than any words or acts of violence.

No one really knows how the story of Adele spread through the village, but the gossip mill is in full swing. Everyone expects that Al will ask for a separation. But Al beats the gossips at their game: he appears, head held high, at Sunday Mass, with Adele at his heels. In true Christian style, he appears to have understood the words of the Our Father: "Forgive us our trespasses as we forgive those who trespass against us." But the forgiveness on which Al prides himself secretly feeds on Adele's humiliation.

At home, Al continues to stoke the flame of his rancour, with silence and furtive, disdainful glances at the sinner. Yet, in heaven, this virtuous posturing fools no one. An angel is sent out to redress the situation. Each time Al casts his harsh and somber gaze on Adele, the angel drops a stone the size of a button on his heart. Each time, Al feels the tinge, his face contorting with pain. His heart gets heavier and heavier, to the point where he ends up having to walk doubled over, painfully stretching out his neck to see ahead.

One day, while Al is swathing his wheat, he notices a radiant personage leaning against the fence, and hears him say: "Al, you seem rather overburdened." Surprised to hear his name on the lips of a stranger, Al asks who he is and how this is any of his business. The angel answers: "I know your wife cheated on you and that the humiliation is torturing you. But the subtle revenge you are inflicting on her is depressing you." Knowing that he has been found out, Al lowers his head and admits: "I can't chase this miserable thought from my mind: how could she have betrayed me—me, such a faithful and generous husband? She's nothing but a slut; she has defiled our bed!" At these words, Al grimaces in pain. The angel offers to help him but Al is convinced that no one can relieve him of his burden. "As powerful as you may be, stranger, you will never be able to erase what has happened."

"You're right, Al. No one can change the past, but you have the power, as of this moment, to see it differently. Recognize your hurt, accept your anger and humiliation. Then, slowly, start to change your outlook on Adele. Is she the only guilty one? Remember how indifferent you were towards her. Put yourself in her shoes. You need new and magic eyes to see your suffering in a different light."

Al does not really understand, but he trusts the angel. He has no other choice; nothing else has worked. He asks his visitor how to change his outlook. The angel instructs him as follows: "Before you look at Adele, smooth out the wrinkles on your forehead, around your mouth and the other muscles in your face. Instead of seeing Adele as a mean woman, look at the wife who needed tenderness; remember how coolly and harshly you treated her; remember her generosity and her warmth that you so loved at the beginning of your relationship. Each time you look at her with these new eyes, I will remove a stone from your heart." Al accepts the deal but not without protesting that he feels awkward. Little by little, slowly and with great effort, he works at seeing Adele through new eyes. Little by little, the pain in his heart eases. Adele seems to change before him: from the unfaithful wife, she becomes the gentle and loving person he had known when they first fell in love. Adele feels the change. Relieved, she regains her high spirits, her smile and her bubbliness. Al, in turn, feels completely different. He lets his heart, still battered by the burden it had carried, be filled with a profound tenderness. The new emotion that overcomes him still scares him. But, one night, he finds himself in tears as, wordlessly, he takes Adele into his arms. The miracle of forgiveness has just taken place.

CHAPTER 3

Unmasking False Notions of Forgiveness

We forgive too little and we forget too much.

— MADAME SWETCHINE

The journey of forgiveness requires both a good memory and a clear awareness of the offence.

Before we can even dream of forgiving, we must get rid of our false notions about forgiveness. In what is left of our Christian culture, certain values have been distorted by popular misinterpretations. Forgiveness is no exception. Even worse are the "spiritual directors" who perpetuate false notions about forgiveness through the written and spoken word. This is an unfortunate state of affairs, given that forgiveness and love of other people, especially of our enemies, are central to the teachings of the Christian gospel and other spiritual traditions: thus the urgency to expose our false notions of both forgiveness and its use. By understanding what is false in the psychological and spiritual dead ends that have grown up around forgiveness, we can avoid discouragement, injustice, spiritual illusion, self-betrayals, and stunted or blocked human and religious growth.

As you read this chapter, perhaps some of your ideas about forgiveness and its practice will be shaken up. In the workshops I have given on the subject, many participants have found themselves making the painful discovery that for many years they had been wrong about the nature of forgiveness. We cannot build a new structure without first clearing the ground and digging a solid foundation.

FORGIVING IS NOT FORGETTING

How often have we heard people say: "I can't forgive him because I can't forget," or "Forget about it," "Turn a new page," "Don't

People who say: "I forgive but I do not forget" show sound mental health.

get stuck in this offence, get on with your life"? These approaches are dead ends for a simple reason. Even if it were possible, forgetting the unfortunate incident would interfere with forgiving because we would no longer know what we were forgiving. If forgiving means forgetting, what happens to those gifted with excellent memories? They would be incapable of forgiveness! The journey of forgiveness requires both a good memory and a clear awareness of the offence; otherwise, the radical change of heart required for forgiveness would be impossible.

It is a mistake to make forgetting the litmus test of forgiving when the opposite is true. Forgiveness helps heal the memory. With forgiveness, the memory of the hurt loses some of its toxicity. The unfortunate event can fade and become less of an obsession; gradually the wound scars over; recalling the offence no longer brings such pain. Thus healed, the memory is no longer preoccupied with depressing thoughts about the offence.

So, people who say: "I forgive but I do not forget" show sound mental health. They understand that forgiveness does not demand they forget the offence. On the other hand, if this is their way of saying they have decided never to trust again and to remain forever on their guard, their process of forgiveness has not run its full course.

FORGIVENESS IS NOT DENIAL

When we are hit hard, one of our most frequent reactions is to build a wall to protect us against pain and our other emotions. This defence reaction often appears as a denial of the offence. If the defence reaction persists, it can eventually become pathological. In such cases, people feel stressed; their emotions are frozen; most of the time, they are not aware of what is happening to

Forgiveness that requires the repression or amputation of a part of the self strikes me as very dangerous.

them. Often, they do not even feel the need, let alone the desire, to heal – and certainly not to forgive. Obviously the alchemy of forgiveness will not work as long as the victim refuses to recognize the offence and the resulting suffering.

Yet, to my great surprise, I have met spiritual directors who do not see denial as an obstacle to but, rather, as the only path to forgiveness. Edith Stauffer is one example among many. In *Unconditional Love and Forgiveness*, she draws on the Essene code of conduct to define forgiveness: "To forgive is to cancel all requirements, conditions and expectations held in the mind that block off the attitude of love" (1987: 113). Does she mean that, to forgive, we must first deny part of ourselves? Such a form of forgiveness, it seems, is nothing but psychological repression. Even if it is motivated by unconditional love, forgiveness that requires the repression or amputation of a part of the self strikes me as very dangerous.

This overly spiritualistic approach to forgiveness fails to take emotions into account. Pauline's case showed me some of its harmful effects. Pauline displayed all the symptoms of depression: stress, anxiety, insomnia, loss of appetite, guilt feelings. She lived with her children in a small town, where her husband freely flaunted his young mistress. This deeply humiliated Pauline and her children. To add insult to injury, the husband had cleaned out the family bank account to pay for his extravagant lifestyle with his new friend. When I questioned Pauline about her emotional state, she immediately answered that, thanks to the writings of a spiritual guide, she had forgiven her husband. On the advice of this guide she had forced herself to inundate her husband with "positive energies" to counter her own "negative" emotions. Among these, anger was the one most likely to destroy her. I had no choice but to contradict her guide's advice and to strongly encourage her to pay attention

Some of our teachers brandished forgiveness as a magic formula capable of righting all wrongs.

to both her shame and her anger, and to find appropriate ways of expressing them. Pauline understood that she had not yet reached the point where she could forgive. She would first have to respect her emotions. On my advice, she found a way to deal with her shame and anger: while cleaning the house, she would beat the carpet as much to get rid of her surplus of adrenaline as to clean it. By gradually accepting her anger, and then the shame of having been publicly humiliated by her husband, Pauline freed herself of her debilitating anxiety attacks and guilt feelings.

FORGIVENESS TAKES MORE THAN WILLPOWER

Let's take two familiar situations. The first one: you tell your son to seek forgiveness from his sister for having gone through her diary and for teasing her about her infatuations. The second: a teacher breaks up an argument between two children in the schoolyard and forces them to forgive each other then and there. Our first sense of forgiveness is born of such childhood experiences. Some of our teachers brandished forgiveness as a magic formula capable of righting all wrongs. With no regard for a child's emotional state, they reduced forgiveness to a simple act of will capable of settling all conflicts instantly and definitively. At that age, we never thought to doubt the value of such an artificial form of forgiving. The words came out of our mouths, but our hearts were not in them. Such forgiveness likely did more to soothe the teacher's nerves than to educate the child.

It is hard to escape the magical, instant – and illusory – forgiveness of our childhood that gave us such a feeling of omnipotence over our emotional world! Inevitably we later become disillusioned. Disappointment and even guilt follow as we find ourselves unable to reproduce the magic. The mistake was in turning forgiveness into a simple act of will instead of making it the culmination of a learning experience. This process takes time; the amount of time depends on the hurt, the offender's reactions, and the resources of the person who was hurt. Will is, of course, a big part of the picture, but alone it cannot do the job of forgiveness. Forgiveness mobilizes all of our faculties: sensitivity, the heart, intelligence, judgment, imagination, and so on.

FORGIVENESS CANNOT BE GIVEN ON COMMAND

Either forgiveness is free or it does not exist. But there is a strong temptation, especially among some preachers, to force people to forgive freely. One day, I was listening to a bishop who was giving the homily in a televised Sunday Mass. He started off on the right track, explaining that forgiveness was a sublime act of generosity as well as a form of transcendence. But as he stressed the Christian "obligation" to forgive, he started to get off track. Interspersed throughout his homily were such expressions as "we *must* forgive," "we *must* forgive others," "the *commandment* about loving your neighbour," and "the Christian *precept*." The cameras sweeping over the audience caught people fidgeting rather uncomfortably. One could only guess at their inner turmoil as the desire to forgive collided with the hesitation brought on by their feelings and emotions that were also clamouring to be heard.

It is not advisable to reduce forgiveness, or any other spiritual practice, to a moral obligation. If we do that, we inevitably rob forgiveness of its free and spontaneous character. Yet, some Christian practitioners advocate this approach. The most obvious example lies with those Christians who, each day, recite the Our Father without realizing that a false interpretation of "Forgive us our trespasses as we forgive those who have trespassed against us"

We often confuse forgiving and reconciling, as if the act of forgiving consisted of re-establishing relationships just as they were before.

assimilates forgiveness into an act of justice on command. They think that they must perform an act of forgiveness before God will forgive them. They forget that God's forgiveness is not conditioned by puny human acts of forgiveness. How sad their view of God seems to be: a calculating and mercenary being, driven by the law of give and take.

There is more. The Our Father's "obligation" to forgive would imply that the person who fails to forgive will be punished by being denied forgiveness. This approach seems to set us back in the mode of the Old Testament *lex talionis*, rather than place us within the spontaneous and free circle of love of the Beatitudes. Personally, to avoid any possible ambiguity in the formula "Forgive us our trespasses as . . . ," I recite it thinking of St. Paul's words: "you must forgive as the Lord forgave you" (Colossians 3.13). In the same vein, a friend told me of her preference for the following: "Forgive us our trespasses so that we may forgive those who have trespassed against us."

FORGIVENESS DOES NOT TAKE US BACK TO WHERE WE WERE BEFORE THE OFFENCE

When I told a psychologist friend of mine that I was writing a book about forgiveness, she became very thoughtful. She admitted that she felt herself unable to forgive a friend who had betrayed her trust by revealing some of her confidences: "I can't forgive her, and I don't think I can go back to being friends with her like before." In her mind, forgiveness meant reconciling, and reconciling meant "going back to where you were before." We often confuse forgiving and reconciling, as if the act of forgiving consisted of re-establishing relationships just as they were before the incident. In close family relationships, communal life and working relationships, reconciliation should be the normal out-

In and of itself, forgiveness is not synonymous with reconciliation.

come of forgiving. But in and of itself, forgiveness is not synonymous with reconciliation; it can stand on its own outside the context of reconciliation.

We can forgive a person who is absent, whether dead or unknown, for instance. Obviously, reconciliation is impossible in such cases. I have known parents who have forgiven their daughter's murderer without ever seeing or knowing the person. In bereavement therapy, it is common practice to ask the bereaved person to forgive the loved one who has gone away. In cases of abuse or violence, the victim is advised to put an end to the relationship with the aggressor to protect him- or herself. This does not mean that forgiveness should be dismissed outright as an option for the future.

It would be wrong to think that once forgiveness has been granted, our relationship with the offender can return to the way it was before the offence. After you've made an omelet, can you retrieve the eggs? And when you've baked a loaf of bread, can you recover the flour? It is impossible to go back after we've been wronged. Either we try to make ourselves believe that nothing happened, in which case we re-establish the relationship in the context of a lie, or we take advantage of the conflict to review the quality of the relationship and re-establish it on more solid footing.

FORGIVENESS DOES NOT MEAN GIVING UP OUR RIGHTS

Following a conference where I talked about forgiveness as an important step in the dynamics of bereavement, a woman came up to me and said: "You should be more careful when you talk about forgiveness. It's dangerous, it's repulsive, to forgive criminals, especially sexual molesters. Doesn't it just encourage them to repeat their offences?" For many people, as for this woman, forgiveness means giving up one's rights and all the demands of justice. Such "forgiveness" would end up encouraging offenders and tyrants to perpetuate their wrongdoings. George Bernard Shaw once said of forgiveness that it was the "haven of crooks." Christians are sometimes accused of doing the same thing, of equating forgiveness with abdicating the requirements of justice, especially when they "turn the other cheek" a bit too readily.

This touches on the whole issue of the relationship between justice and forgiveness. Addressing all aspects of the question would take us too far off-topic. Let's just say that while justice concerns itself with re-establishing the rights of an injured party on an objective basis, forgiveness depends primarily on freely expressed goodwill. This does not mean that, by forgiving, we abandon the need for justice. I tried to explain this to a woman who wrote me to say that her husband was asking for a divorce and was refusing to give her any type of compensation for her twenty years of marriage and work. Despite this obvious injustice, she was ready to forgive him everything. "Even though I have brought up the children and contributed to the success of his diplomatic career, I do not wish him ill. I forgive him for having abandoned me without a penny, for wanting to take away my children and even for having rejected me for a younger woman." In my view, such an attitude, as beautiful and generous as it may appear, hides a great deal of fear and cowardice towards the "great man." I answered her this way: "You are confusing forgiveness and justice. Get yourself a good lawyer. Exercise your rights. Then you can decide whether you still want to forgive him." And she did just that.

Forgiveness that does not fight injustice, far from being a sign of strength and courage, shows weakness and false tolerance. It encourages the offender to repeat the crime. This is

False excuses often serve as clever and well-camouflaged tricks for reducing our suffering.

what some bishops failed to understand when they did not intervene quickly or decisively after having been told about the sexual abuse committed by certain members of the clergy.

FORGIVENESS DOES NOT MEAN EXCUSING THE OFFENDER

"I forgive him, it's not his fault." This is another false conception of forgiveness. False, because forgiving someone is not the same as excusing them; excusing them means absolving them of all moral responsibility. There is no limit to the number of pretexts used for these excuses: heredity, education, and prevailing culture are among them. At this rate, no one would be responsible for their actions since no one would be free enough. This is a warped interpretation of the saying "To understand all is to forgive all." We may as well just whitewash all crimes if we believe this view of forgiveness.

False excuses often serve as clever and well-camouflaged tricks for reducing our suffering. Convincing ourselves that the offender is not responsible is easier to deal with than accepting that he or she inflicted the injury consciously and freely. The ready excuse can become a double-edged sword. Although on the one hand it provides relief, on the other it shows low regard and disdain for the offender. It quietly states: "You're not smart enough to be responsible for such a misdeed." As a result, it humiliates more than it liberates. Gabriel Marcel illustrates this point well in his play *La grâce*. Françoise, an unfaithful wife, can no longer handle her husband Gerard's hopeless efforts to excuse her. He tells her: "I don't have to forgive you ... the reasons behind your actions are beyond your control." Françoise, humiliated, protests: "No, not this! ... I would rather be dead!" (Davy 1959: 115).

Authentic forgiveness from the heart stems from humility, and opens the path to genuine reconciliation.

FORGIVENESS DOES NOT DEMONSTRATE MORAL SUPERIORITY

Some acts of forgiveness humiliate more than they liberate. In these cases, forgiveness can become a subtle gesture of moral grandstanding, of "supreme arrogance," according to one author. Under the guise of magnanimity, it may hide an instinctive grasp for power. How do we explain that those granting forgiveness sometimes assume airs of false superiority? It amounts to them trying to hide their profound humiliation. Overcome by shame and rejection, they try to protect themselves. They try to cover up their humiliation by playing the wronged but generous and merciful lord.

There is a strong temptation to forgive in order to dazzle the onlookers. In one fell swoop, the offended party grants forgiveness as much to show his or her moral superiority as to expose the offender's inferiority. When forgiveness is used this way, it is obviously nothing more than a caricature of its reality. Authentic forgiveness from the heart stems from humility, and opens the path to genuine reconciliation. False forgiveness does nothing but perpetuate the dominator–dominated relationship. It is in protest of this haughty form of forgiveness that Edmée, a character in Gabriel Marcel's play *A Man of God*, speaks out. Edmée had cheated on her husband, a Protestant pastor. After being subjected to his haughty forgiveness for years, she can take it no longer and cries out: "This cheap grandiosity of spirit makes me sick." To which Claude replies: "Cheap? Why, when I forgave you ... " Edmée interrupts: "If you did not forgive me because you loved me, what am I to make of your forgiveness?" (Davy 1959: 142).

Forgiveness that serves only to show moral superiority is practised by three types of "professional" forgivers. First, there are the compulsive ones who bombard others with forgiveness

Far from being a manifestation of power, real forgiveness is first and foremost an act of inner strength.

at the slightest trifle. Then there are the guilt chasers. They aggravate a situation so they can show leniency and impress others with their forgiveness. Third, there are the perpetual victims, of which the most common examples are wives of alcoholic husbands. They expect to get sympathy and admiration from their acquaintances because they have sacrificed their lives to these men and constantly forgive them each time they get drunk.

Far from being a manifestation of power, real forgiveness is first and foremost an act of inner strength. We need inner strength to recognize and accept our vulnerability, rather than camouflage it with the appearance of benevolence. Initially we may be swayed by the need to show our superiority through the act of forgiving. But in the course of forgiveness, those granting forgiveness will be given many opportunities to purify any motives that may taint their efforts.

FORGIVENESS DOES NOT
MEAN LEAVING IT TO GOD

"Only God can forgive." No doubt you have heard this line spoken as if human beings had no place in the act of forgiving. This makes a nice pretext for passing all of one's responsibilities on to God! But it would be wrong to do so, since in the realm of forgiveness, as in any other, God doesn't do for us what is up to us to do. Recently, someone was telling me how easy it was for them to forgive: "If someone hurts me, I quickly ask God to forgive them. That way, I don't have to be disturbed by all sorts of feelings of pain, resentment or humiliation." As admirable as this demonstration of faith may be, it raises questions about the mental health of the individual who is doing the forgiving. Instead of taking charge of

Forgiveness depends as much on human as on divine actions.

life, as painful as this may be, the person hands it over to God. Don't misunderstand me: while I believe that the spiritual is an essential element of forgiveness, I also believe that we have to prepare ourselves to receive God's grace on the human plane first. Forgiveness depends as much on human as on divine actions. Nature and grace do not counteract each other, but are coordinated and complementary.

Such caricatures of forgiveness are very real. In *Is Human Forgiveness Possible?*, John Patton sees the travesties of forgiveness as serious enough to make him despair of the possibility of human forgiveness. He thinks it would be better to defer entirely to God, who alone can forgive. This is why, instead of desperately trying to forgive, those who have been offended should concentrate their energies on becoming conscious of "forgiveness already granted by him" (1985: 120). To me, Patton's position seems exaggerated and untenable, for it fails to take into account the contribution of human forgiveness, as humble as it may be.

At this point, let us remember that even though setting out on the road to real forgiveness may require a great deal of courage, avoiding giving in to the mirage of false forgiveness requires just as much.

The Great Paradoxes of Forgiveness
Easy but often inaccessible
Available but often forgotten
Liberating for the other and even more so for ourselves
On everyone's lips and yet misunderstood
Innate to the human heart and yet illusory
Vital for humans but so often feared
Bestowed upon the soul and yet menacing
Mysterious and yet an everyday occurrence
Utterly divine and utterly human

CHAPTER 4

Forgiveness – A Human and Spiritual Adventure

Forgiveness is the sublime on a daily basis.
— VLADIMIR JANKELEVITCH

The process of forgiveness calls upon all our faculties.

Once upon a time, two countries were at war. One day, a rumour began: the enemy camp had just acquired an awesome weapon. Blind people were sent to the other camp to spy on the secret weapon. Their handicap allowed them to get close to the new war engine without arousing any suspicion. They found themselves feeling a huge elephant. Upon their return to camp, each one delivered his report. The first spy, who had explored the ear, said: "It's a rough object, large and flexible like a carpet." The second one, who had felt the trunk, objected: "Not at all. It's more like an empty pipe." The third, who had examined the leg, claimed, in turn, that it was a large, solid pillar. And so it went, as each one gave a report contradicting what the others had said.

You guessed it. It's as incongruous to describe forgiveness by one of its aspects as to reduce the description of an elephant to one of its parts. I leave it to my readers to determine whether I have done better than my predecessors in describing the essential components of forgiveness.

The term "forgiveness," as it is frequently used in everyday conversation, is misleading because it does not convey the complex reality that is intended. Most of the time, it ends up being described as a willful act isolated from its context. But real forgiveness is more than that! For one thing, it is more than an act of willpower. The process of forgiveness calls

45

The first step on the long road to forgiveness is the decision to not seek revenge.

upon all our faculties. Furthermore, forgiveness is never instantaneous. Because it is comprised of a before, during and after, it must be spread out over time.

The act of forgiving therefore needs a whole set of conditions, each as necessary as the others: it takes time; we must be patient with the process; we must restrain our desire for efficiency, and persevere in our decision to see the process through to the end. The most appropriate expressions I can find to describe it are: "inner conversion," "pilgrimage of the heart," "an introduction to loving your enemies," "quest for inner freedom." All of these expressions reflect the need for a process.

Here, in their broadest strokes, are what I consider the main components of forgiveness.

THE STARTING POINT: DECIDING NOT TO SEEK REVENGE

"The longest journey starts with a single step." The first step on the long road to forgiveness is the decision to not seek revenge. We do not make this decision out of grim determination, but because we want to heal and grow.

It is useless to go back over all the heartbreaks and miseries that revenge has wrought on our world. They are serious enough that we should not allow ourselves to be tempted by this "descent into hell" even as our instinct naturally pulls us in that direction. The great French historian Jean Delumeau commented, using the words of a Cuban poet imprisoned in the jails of Fidel Castro for 22 years: "For him, forgiving means breaking the spiral of violence, refusing to fight with the hateful weapons of your adversary, retaining or recapturing your freedom even while you are in chains" (Perrin 1987:

To free our offender, we must first be free ourselves.

214). In the same vein, Jacques-Marie Pohier wrote, "What does pardon consist of? Not making someone pay." As negative as this definition may be, it is nonetheless true that the decision to not seek revenge is the starting point for any real forgiveness.

GOING BACK INTO OURSELVES

When someone hurts us, we feel troubled; we panic. An offence shakes our peace and harmony, shatters our tranquility and threatens our inner integrity. Carefully hidden personal deficiencies suddenly surface. Our ideals, if not illusions, of tolerance and generosity are put to the test. The shadow side of our personality emerges. Emotions that we had thought were under control run amok. The confusion leaves us powerless and humiliated. Old, improperly healed wounds re-open and demand attention.

Thus, the temptation to refuse to become aware of and accept our inner weakness is great. We use various tactics to avoid this awareness and acceptance: we deny, we try to forget, we escape into activity, we play the victim, we waste energy trying to find the guilty party; we seek punishment that fits the crime; we blame ourselves to the point of depression; we build a shell around ourselves, or play the untouchable or benevolent hero.

Giving in to such temptations compromises the outcome of the process of forgiveness. To free our offender, we must first be free ourselves. Some literature on forgiveness — in particular, New Age writing on the topic — advises forgiving without taking our own mental state into account. This is poor advice, since to forgive, we must become self-aware and discover our inner poverty: shame, aggressivity, vengefulness, a

Forgiveness turns the situation around, creating a new relationship with the offender.

sense of rejection and a desire to just get it over with. Looking at ourselves more lucidly and more honestly brings us to a full stop on the winding road to forgiveness. Initially, such self-examination can be frightening or discouraging. But difficult as it may be, it is essential, since before we can forgive another, we must forgive ourselves.

LOOKING FOR A NEW VISION OF HUMAN RELATIONSHIPS

The French theologian Christian Duquoc calls forgiveness "an invitation to the imagination." There is no better way of putting it, for imagination plays an essential role in the process of forgiving. Duquoc continues: "It is forgiveness that represents this innovative gesture: it creates a space in which the logic inherent in legal equivalences no longer runs. Forgiveness is not a forgetfulness of the past, it is the risk of a future other than the one imposed by the past or by memory" (1986: 55). Therefore, to take the path of forgiveness, it is important to dream of a better world where justice and compassion prevail. Utopia? Not at all. Every new world begins with our wildest dreams.

Forgiveness, therefore, is part of how we see the world. It is, in part, the desire to create or, better yet, to recreate. Miguel Rubio captured the originality of this idea: "Forgiving is neither a common, routine gesture, nor an everyday habit. Rather, it is a hidden, original flower that blooms anew each time from the soil of pain and self-control" (1986: 101). Creation, after all, is the act of making something out of nothing. Forgiveness springs up from the "nothing" of want or the emptiness that the wrong has introduced into a human relationship. Forgiveness turns the situation around,

To be able to forgive, we must continue to believe in the dignity of the person who hurt, oppressed or betrayed us.

creating a new relationship with the offender. Released from their painful links with the past, those who forgive can allow themselves to live the present to its fullest and to envisage a new relationship with the offender.

At this point, having learned to set aside bad feelings, we can start seeing through new lenses. Psychotherapy calls this "reframing." Reframing situates the offence in a larger context. Until that point, we focused solely on the wound, blinded to anything else by our bitterness. When we look at the big picture in a fairer and larger frame of reference, our perspective and our horizon broaden. The offence that took up such an over-whelming amount of space starts to lose its importance in the face of the new possibilities for being and behaving. But the work of forgiving doesn't end here.

BANKING ON THE VALUE OF THE OFFENDER

To be able to forgive, we must continue to believe in the dignity of the person who hurt, oppressed or betrayed us. Naturally, at first, this is very hard to do. The offender comes across as a malicious character who deserves to be condemned.

But, once healing takes place, as in the story of Al and Adele, our vision of the other as evil may change. Behind the monster, we discover a fragile and weak person like ourselves, someone capable of changing and evolving.

Forgiveness not only lifts the weight of pain from our hearts, but also frees the other from the burden of our spiteful and severe judgment; it restores their human dignity. Jean Delumeau puts it well: "Forgiveness is liberation, deliverance, and re-creation. It makes us new. (...) It restores joy and freedom to those staggering under the weight of their guilt. Forgiveness (...) is an act of trust in relation to a human

49

Authentic forgiveness insists that we overcome our fear of being humiliated yet again.

being; it is our saying 'yes' to our sister or brother" (Perrin 1987: 3). Similarly, the Latin American theologian Jon Sobrino sees forgiveness as an act of love towards our enemy, an act that can change that enemy: "Forgiving someone who has offended us is an act of love towards the sinner whom we wish to release from their own unhappiness, and whose future we do not wish to close off entirely" (1986: 59).

This is all very well and good, you might say, but isn't it always risky to want to go that far? Won't the offender just withdraw into their shell and refuse the freedom we are offering? Will we be hurt a second time by their refusal of our forgiveness? Certainly the risk is real. Is it worth taking? Authentic forgiveness insists that we overcome our fear of being humiliated yet again. Jacques-Marie Pohier addresses this fear: "This is why forgiveness is difficult. Because we are scared" (1977: 215).

REFLECTING DIVINE MERCY

At this point, we can rightfully ask if the act of forgiveness lies beyond mere human strength.

Forgiveness belongs to two worlds: the human and the divine. In conceiving of forgiveness, we must avoid two main errors. We must not reduce it purely and simply to human behaviour driven by fear or pity. A behavioural psychologist who equates forgiveness with a defensive tactic sees forgiveness among humans as prompted by fear of retaliation and mutual destruction. The Roman philosopher Seneca sees pity as the main motivator for forgiveness. He summarizes his thoughts in this famous formula: "Forgive those who are weaker than you out of pity for them; forgive those who are stronger than you out of pity for yourself."

Forgiveness stands at the crossroads between the human and the spiritual.

The other error, which I already mentioned, is to consider forgiveness as the prerogative of God alone. When we proclaim without nuance that "God alone can forgive" or "Forgiveness is the realm of God," we leave little room for human responsibility. Certainly, forgiveness is the "realm of God" if we mean, as do the Jewish, Christian and Muslim traditions, that God is the ultimate source of true forgiveness. But forgiveness cannot happen without human cooperation.

Forgiveness stands at the crossroads between the human and the spiritual. It is important to respect these two components so we can express them properly; otherwise, we risk cutting forgiveness off from one or another of its essential elements. Again, Jean Delumeau has captured this point: "[Forgiveness] constitutes the only possible link between human beings, and between human beings and God. (…) The rainbow between God and humanity is forgiveness" (Perrin 1987: 5).

Up to this point, we have examined the human responsibilities in matters of forgiveness: deciding not to seek revenge, looking after our own healing, creating a new order and, finally, freeing our brother or sister. These tasks already seem to be well beyond what humans can handle – with good reason, since the term "to forgive," its etymology suggests, means giving in abundance, just as "to perfect" means doing in abundance. Forgiveness incorporates this idea of abundance since it expresses a form of love taken to the extreme: loving in spite of the offence suffered. Accomplishing this requires spiritual strength that goes well beyond human strength.

The spiritual experience that we live out in the process of forgiveness belongs to another order of being and acting. At this level, the ego must be prepared to abandon personal

Forgiveness is a real challenge.

control of the situation. In other words, to enter into the ultimate phase of forgiveness, we must be open to the unknown and unexpected.

Thanks to this "active passivity," we will become attentive to the action of the Spirit who breathes where and when it wants. Then, patient and determined psychological work gives way to relaxed waiting, filled with the hope for a forgiveness that comes, not from ourselves, but from an Other.

Giving up our desire for power – that is, wanting to be the only means of forgiveness – takes us further than we might expect. My research has convinced me that, to succeed in the act of forgiveness, we must be detached from the very desire to forgive. How gratifying it would be to be able to declare triumphantly: "I forgive you." Yet in its ultimate expression, forgiveness knows no such fulfillment. Discreet, humble, even silent, it belongs neither to the realm of feeling nor to that of emotion. Rather, it emerges from the depth of the being, from the heart animated by the Spirit. Lewis Smedes thinks that forgiveness possesses a particular quality that has nothing to do with sentimentality. Rather, forgiveness has feeling, colour and ambiance, all of which make it different from any other act of creation in the range of human relations (1984: 38).

Forgiveness is a real challenge, the challenge of maintaining the tension between the psychological and the spiritual. A complete and enlightened overview of forgiveness must, therefore, take this challenge into account. This is what I have tried to achieve by spreading the process of forgiveness over twelve steps.

To close this chapter, I would like to share with you a text by Philippe le Touzé, who describes beautifully God's creative

Forgiveness is God himself.

activity in forgiveness. He describes the characters in the works of Georges Bernanos, known as the prophet of forgiveness: "The saints of Bernanos descend into the canyon of this 'gentle pity'. Forgiveness is God himself, the merciful father of the prodigal son, love in its purest gratuitousness. Love is creative, spreads beyond itself, and forgiveness is the instrument of continuous, restored and renewed creation. Where human beings engender death, forgiveness births life" (Perrin 1987: 237).

CHAPTER 5

Assessing the Offence

As long as we love, we forgive. — HONORÉ DE BALZAC

Not only is there such a thing as false forgiveness, but there are also false motives for forgiveness.

"Father, after thinking about it, I've decided to write you to forgive you for failing me in my last exam," wrote one of my former students. I was stunned by her naïveté and offhandedness. I did not understand why I should be forgiven for a failure that she had brought upon herself. At that moment I understood that not only is there such a thing as false forgiveness, but that there are also false motives for forgiveness. As in this case, we run the risk of cheapening forgiveness and invoking it in bad faith. Hence we need to distinguish clearly between those circumstances that call for forgiveness and those that have nothing to do with this fine spiritual practice.

In some situations, forgiveness has no place since we get what our actions deserve. I'm speeding and I get a ticket; I gamble at the casino and I lose; I come in late too often and my boss reprimands me. In each instance, I'm frustrated and angry, and my pride is wounded. But will the professor, the police officer, the croupier or the boss ask forgiveness for humiliation I've brought on myself? Clearly not. Forgiveness must be given only when the offence is not justified: if the police officer had shouted at me, the croupier had cheated me, or the boss had publicly humiliated me.

WHEN THE OFFENDER IS SOMEONE YOU LOVE

Forgiveness takes on different colours and forms depending on whether we are dealing with close relatives or friends, or with

Forgiveness takes on different colours and forms depending on whether we are dealing with close relatives or friends, or with strangers.

strangers. Who can hurt us more deeply than our loved ones, with whom we have created bonds of affection? In a way, they are a part of us. We idealize them and, consequently, we raise our expectations of them. This is why the seriousness of the injury is measured less by the objective seriousness of the offence than by our expectations – realistic or not – of the person.

There are many cases of unreasonable expectations. Children idealize their parents and demand unconditional tolerance and love from them. On the other hand, most parents expect their children to fit perfectly into their way of thinking and to fulfill their own broken dreams. Romantic love is equally fraught with unrealistic dreams. Spouses and lovers hope that their partners will guess their every desire without ever having to articulate them. They want their partners to love, understand, appreciate, and make them feel secure by their constant presence. I shall spare you the list of expectations and implicit hopes entertained by lovers, parents, children, sisters, brothers and friends. It is important to remember that forgiveness plays an indispensable part in intimate relationships because they are so intense and they present so many opportunities for misunderstanding.

Of course, we must be careful not to exaggerate small, everyday annoyances and disappointments. A wife comes home late for supper; a husband forgets his wife's birthday; a child muddies a freshly washed floor; the last one who used the family car didn't bother to fill it up with gas. When these things happen, we may feel disappointed, frustrated, or even hostile. We should neither give such incidents too much importance nor ignore them entirely. They may point to a problem in the relationship that we should look into and resolve, perhaps through forgiveness. This would be the case if,

Nothing is quite as painful as learning that we have been betrayed by someone we hold in high regard.

after discussing the incidents with those who committed them, the latter failed to change their behaviour.

Sometimes, insignificant everyday events may have serious consequences. A surgeon told me that he was thinking of divorcing his new wife because she was a night owl who, when she came to bed, disturbed his much-needed sleep. Sometimes she would feel the need to chat in the wee hours, especially if there was a misunderstanding to straighten out. He needed a full night's rest to maintain his concentration and steady hand. He had come to despise his wife to the point of thinking that she wanted to ruin him professionally.

There are even more serious examples of lack of consideration. Just think of the betrayals and infidelities between people who should love each other. Their failures lead to painful and lasting wounds, since we tend to think that parents, friends and colleagues will naturally make the best of it, no matter what. They have an unspoken agreement to provide each other with mutual protection, whether the other is present or not. This is why I was at once hurt and disturbed by an old friend's indiscretion towards me. In a private conversation, I had confided to him a secret that he soon passed on to someone whom, to make matters worse, I didn't like very much. I must confess that I have not had the courage to ask him to explain his indiscretion, so our friendship has been severely damaged.

What can we say about betrayals? Nothing is quite as painful as learning that we have been betrayed by someone we hold in high regard: a friend who talks about us behind our back; the spouse who cheats on us with one of our friends; the colleague who grabs power at our expense.

Other instances of disloyalty towards intimates, such as ridicule and sarcasm, are more subtle but no less hurtful. They

The closer the offence hits, the more it shatters us.

are always hard to endure, even for bystanders. I must admit that I feel very uncomfortable when I witness public fights between couples: the wife who comments on her husband's poor sexual performance; the husband who enjoys pointing out his foreign-born wife's mistakes in English. Such scenes become unbearable for the witnesses – not to mention the spouse who is being humiliated!

There is no doubt that acts of violence between people who have sworn to love each other can be counted among the cruelest and most reprehensible of offences. Statistics indicate that many women are abused by their husbands or partners. These statistics do not show the verbal and psychological abuse that preceded the blows. And what are we to make of the epidemic of sexual abuse inflicted by parents on their children, which society has finally decided to make public?

Thus far we have been talking about serious failures in loving those who are close to us. At first glance, other situations may not seem to need forgiveness, because the pain associated with them was not inflicted intentionally. Sometimes, for instance, we do not realize how often the decision of a child to leave home to live with a partner or get married causes much more pain than parents let on.

The separation caused by death awakens a host of feelings, among them fear, pain, anger and guilt. This is why, during grief therapy sessions, I invite survivors to perform a ritual of forgiveness to overcome their anger and guilt feelings. By asking forgiveness of their departed loved one, they can stop reproaching themselves for not having loved that person better; by forgiving them, they eliminate any residual anger at having been abandoned.

Poorly healed childhood memories can aggravate the seriousness of the injury.

WHEN THE OFFENDER IS A STRANGER

A reckless driver cuts you off; a customer in a hurry pushes in front of you at the checkout; a bus driver answers you rudely; you wait in line for the automated banking machine only to have it break down just as your turn comes. Such annoyances do not, of course, require any lengthy procedures of forgiveness. The heat of the moment might produce a slight burst of adrenaline, but we can soon forget such rudeness. After all, the culprits are strangers — or machines!

Therefore, to destroy our inner peace, the actions of a stranger must be more serious. Such actions must strike at our physical, psychological, social or moral integrity. Take, for example, a break-in at our home. Naturally, we deplore the loss of stolen objects, especially if they have sentimental value. Most infuriating is the awareness that our territory has been violated. The closer the offence hits, the more it shatters us: violence against people we love, attacks on our reputation, physical brutality, sexual touching, rape, etc. Our personal safety is jeopardized; our personal boundaries are violated; we are left naked, at someone else's mercy. The ensuing shame and panic constitute a major obstacle to forgiveness, as we shall see later on. We should also be aware that poorly healed childhood memories can aggravate the seriousness of the injury.

The injury inflicted by a stranger becomes more traumatic if we cannot understand the motive behind it. How can you forgive faceless political terrorists who have abducted, tortured and killed members of your family? Francine Crockenpot, a French musician and poet, has tried. After escaping death at the hands of an anonymous attacker, she wanted to establish a rapport with this total stranger. To share

The offence can revive memories and unleash a chain reaction.

her distress with him, she started writing to him, knowing full well that her letters would never reach him: "From the moment of my return, as if to exorcise my panic, I grabbed a pencil and a pad of paper and started to write, up to five or six letters a night, unable to reread what I had written since I had lost an eye. I wrote to my attacker, this stranger I knew nothing about, not even the sound of his voice, since he hadn't even answered me when I cried out: 'But why do you want to kill me?'" (Aggressor 1987: 5).

WHEN THE OFFENCE IS BURIED IN THE PAST

Whether someone we love or a total stranger commits the offence, we must always remember that the offence can revive memories and unleash a chain reaction. Old wounds that we thought were well repressed or concealed reawaken all at once, thereby increasing our panic and confusion. The offence is then seen and magnified through the eyes of the frightened child who lives within each of us.

This happened in the case of the social worker who, during therapy, told me about all the difficulties he was having with his male superiors. He insisted that they were dishonest, which seemed to explain his lack of confidence in them. From time to time, he realized that he was "going too far" and accused himself of being "paranoid." Tired of these perpetual conflicts with management, he asked me to help him discover the root of this mistrust towards his superiors. His ongoing self-examination had yielded nothing but frustration. So I asked him to relive, on the spot, his feelings of mistrust, and, from there, to progressively move back into his past, retracing all his experiences of mistrust towards authority figures. He had to start over several times before he succeeded, since the

In many cases, our inability to forgive goes back to old wounds and childhood deprivations.

original experience was buried deeply. One time when he was trying especially hard, he suddenly started to sob. He had just relived the unhappy event. At age seven, after his tonsils were removed, he woke up from the anaesthetic to find himself alone and in pain in a hospital room. He panicked. His father had promised he would be there when the little boy woke up, and he wasn't. The seven-year-old, alone and miserable, waited all afternoon and all evening – in vain. The surgeon who had promised to bring him ice cream didn't show up either. Only the nurse showed up for a few short visits. The child, feeling thus abandoned, had decided that he would never again trust grown-ups, especially men. After shedding a lot of tears, he finally understood the source of his obsessive mistrust of men in authority. He could then forgive his father and his surgeon for failing to keep their word and could relive other past conflicts with his superiors, and defuse them.

This man's story is far from unique. In many cases, our inability to forgive goes back to old wounds and childhood deprivations.

CHAPTER 6

Who Needs Forgiveness?

*People cannot live together unless they forgive each
other just for being who they are.*

— FRANÇOIS VARILLON

*Intimate
relationships
tend to create
conflicts most
readily.*

Would human relationships become impossible
without forgiveness? Who needs forgiveness?
First, ourselves, then family members, close
friends and acquaintances as well as strangers, institutions,
traditional enemies — and even God. A rather incomplete list
of examples follows.

FORGIVE FAMILY MEMBERS
Since intimate relationships tend to create conflicts most
readily, family members are the most important people to forgive.
You may need to forgive:
- parents who disappointed you once you became aware
  of their shortcomings
- the father who is jealous of your success
- the overprotective mother who won't let you grow
- the absent and silent father
- the sibling who took your place in the family
- the brother who refused to help you when you needed it
- the brother who wouldn't introduce you to his friends
- the alcoholic parent who shamed you
- the incestuous father who destroyed your trust in him
  and in men
- the spouse who changes to the point where you no
  longer recognize them
- the husband whose sexual dalliances humiliated you

When you build up enormous expectations of friends and acquaintances, you may be deeply disappointed.

- the wife who slept with your buddy and humiliated you
- the spouse who put you down
- the spouse who's always trying to dominate you
- the ex-spouse
- the jealous mother-in-law whose son you "stole"
- the father-in-law who made sexual advances to you
- the child who demands more attention than you can give
- the teenager whose delinquent behaviour puts you to shame
- the child who refuses to follow your rules
- the child who doesn't respect your values and destroys your dreams for their future.

The list can go on ...

FORGIVE CLOSE FRIENDS AND ACQUAINTANCES

When you build up enormous expectations of friends and acquaintances, you may be deeply disappointed by:

- the friend who hurt you unfairly
- the friends who let you down when you needed them
- the indiscreet girlfriend who broke your confidence
- the friend who won't acknowledge you when important people are around
- the person you love who abandons you by moving away or dying
- the friend who forgets their promises
- the friend who never confides in you
- the insensitive teachers who made school a waste of time for you
- the boss who humiliates you to make himself look good
- the colleague who puts you down in front of the boss

Forgiving institutions and associations can be rather difficult.

• the supervisor who makes unflattering comments about you in public.

This list can go on, too ...

FORGIVE STRANGERS

Circumstances beyond your control can bring you face to face with individuals who do unexpected harm that we could never foresee:

• the drunk driver who killed your child
• the doctor whose incorrect diagnosis made you lose your time, money and health
• the driver who damaged your car in the parking lot without owning up to it
• the robber who violated the privacy of your home.

This list is not exhaustive either.

FORGIVE INSTITUTIONS

Forgiving institutions and associations can be rather difficult, because they are more anonymous. But you can still offer your forgiveness to their representatives:

• the company that fires you after long years of dedicated service
• the Church that insists on celibacy if you want to be a priest
• police that indiscriminately apply inflexible laws
• the Church that takes forever to grant your annulment
• legislators who make laws favouring the rich.

You can probably name other examples in this category.

We still feel the humiliation from past events which the memories of successive generations have handed on to us.

FORGIVE TRADITIONAL ENEMIES

At first it may seem outrageous to expect that people would forgive a country's long-standing historical enemies. Such a position can be justified by claiming that it is impossible for them to put themselves in the place of the victims. This explanation is hard to defend since nations keep alive the wounds inflicted on their ancestors through a collective memory that maintains prejudices and suspicions about, stirs up hatred against and provokes unjustified attacks on the descendants of those enemies. To the extent that we still feel the humiliation from past events which the memories of successive generations have handed on to us, you must turn to the healing power of forgiveness in situations such as these:

- the nations who conquered your ancestors
- the people who humiliated your people by forbidding them to speak their language and practise their religion
- the conqueror who used assimilation tactics
- the race that committed, or tried to commit, genocide on yours.

Undoubtedly you can add to this list, too.

FORGIVE GOD

Even God can be put on trial. This delicate subject raises the thorny problem of the relationship between the existence of evil in the world and the goodness of God. The issue is too complex to address satisfactorily here. I simply want to say this to those of you who want to deepen your spiritual life and strengthen your capacity to forgive: If we contemplate the God of Jesus Christ, we recognize that God, far from wanting or even allowing evil in this world, is its first victim. In this

*What must
you forgive
yourself for?*

context, I leave you one simple question, to which I am fully aware that I cannot provide an adequate answer: "Which God should we forgive?" The all-powerful God to whom we attribute a great deal of wrong-doing is not the meek and humble God of Jesus Christ.

You may feel the need to forgive God because
• God allows children to suffer and die
• God says he loves you and doesn't help you when you're in trouble
• God is supposed to be everywhere and you don't see him
• God doesn't seem to answer your prayers
• God doesn't give you the happiness you think you deserve because you've carried out all your religious duties
• God took away your beloved, whose love let you taste a bit of heaven here on earth
• God lets abuse happen, even in the Church, and doesn't do anything about it
• God is always judging you
• You can't be as God insists you be.

FORGIVE YOURSELF

Although I left forgiving ourselves to the end of this list, it actually belongs at the beginning. If compassionate acceptance of ourselves and our poverty does not precede forgiveness of another, forgiveness is superficial. What must you forgive yourself for?
• for putting yourself in a situation where you let yourself be hurt
• for not knowing what to do or say
• for falling in love recklessly

- for putting yourself down by buying into your attacker's insults
- for blaming yourself and taking your attacker's side
- for enduring a bad relationship too long
- for feeling vulnerable and wanting to love again
- for being a perfectionist and not letting yourself make mistakes.

You may want to add to this list as you see fit.

CHAPTER 7

An Experience of True Forgiveness

Forgive to free up the force of love that lies within you. — MARTIN GRAY

In forgiveness, as in all other spiritual practices such as meditation or prayer, we cannot improvise.

Reading a book about forgiveness may be very useful, but there's nothing like first-hand experience to deepen understanding. To this end, I'm suggesting here an experience of meditation. In forgiveness, as in all other spiritual practices such as meditation or prayer, we cannot improvise. I really don't know where people get the idea that they could succeed on the first try without any previous experience.

TO FACILITATE A GOOD
EXPERIENCE OF FORGIVENESS

These instructions on the meditation will help this experience turn out well:

1. The most important part of this experience is to follow the movements of your heart closely, to learn about yourself and accept yourself as you are in your journey. First, don't force yourself to forgive at any cost. Forgiveness needs to mature, and will emerge in its own time. If it happens now, fine. If not, that's fine, too. If you find your heart closing off from any compassion, that's all right, too. Accept whatever is happening within you. And, no matter how determined you may be to enter into the experience, give yourself permission to stop as soon as you feel you need to.

2. For this exercise, I recommend you choose a minor offence. Just as you don't start a fitness program by trying to

69

At the end of your meditation, it would be useful to write up your thoughts and feelings in a journal.

lift fifty-kilo weights, or run a marathon, don't start by trying to forgive people who seriously offended you – like the crook who ruined you or the ex-spouse who tormented you for so many years. Instead, choose the rude bus driver, the rebellious teenager or the surly boss.

3. Taping the meditation beforehand could help your concentration.

4. At the end of your meditation, it would be useful to write up your thoughts and feelings in a journal. Sharing them with a partner would be even better, because it will help you deepen your reflections.

5. This meditation lasts about twenty minutes. To ensure that it goes smoothly, eliminate anything that could distract you. Unplug the telephone. The best position is to sit comfortably, with both feet touching the ground and eyes closed.

The Process of Meditation

Take the time to be silent and go into yourself.

Little by little, focus on the movements of your heart.

Feel its beating, its warmth.

Then, ask yourself: "What does forgiveness mean to me? What new quality of life could it bring me?"

Remember a happy experience in which you were forgiven.

Take time to savour the joy of that experience of forgiveness.

Imagine your world made up of happy relationships and forgiveness.

Now, let the memory of the person towards whom you feel resentment rise up in you. See them. Hear them. Continue to truly feel what is happening in you.

Continue to be aware of your own feelings as you let this person whom your heart had rejected get closer to you. Become aware of any blockages that may be welling up in you at this moment.
Let the feelings and emotions that the encounter evokes emerge. Take the time to identify and accept them.

If your feelings are too strong, don't go any further.
Take the time to digest and assimilate them before proceeding.

If you feel all right, continue to let the person whom you wish
to forgive get closer to you. Keep observing what is going on within yourself.

When you feel you are ready, allow that person into your heart. Whisper: "I forgive you." Speak to that person's heart and, in your own words and your own way, repeat softly: "I forgive you for all that you have done in the past, whether or not it was deliberate, to hurt or wrong me: your words, your gestures, or even your thoughts. I forgive you; I forgive you."

Be aware of how much this person may be suffering, frightened or hurt.

Give that person time to receive your forgiveness and to be moved by it.

It is so touching, so awesome, so comforting when two hearts meet in respect and peace!

You will recognize that, for you, the offence is over with, finished, settled, that it has no more hold on you. Forgiveness erases any lingering resentment because your two hearts have joined and offered each other mutual recognition.

With forgiveness, all ends well.

Then give that person your blessing to go on their way, free, transformed, renewed by your forgiveness. Allow them to take their leave, and wish them the greatest possible happiness.

Take time to savour this healing. Thank God for giving you this grace.

AFTER THE MEDITATION
Take some time to reflect so you can reap all the benefits of this meditation. Either share your reflections with someone or write them down in your journal. The following questions may help this process:

What did you experience during the meditation?

If you feel free, congratulate yourself and celebrate this forgiveness.

If you have come up against obstacles, congratulate yourself on your courage and take time to identify the obstacles.

What still gets blocked in you? Take the time to accept this blockage.

What do you need to undo this or these blockages?

What do you need to continue on with the process of forgiveness?

Once you have learned about the various stages you have to go through to forgive (see p. 75), ask yourself which one you have reached.

PART TWO

The Twelve Steps of True Forgiveness

To my knowledge, none of the major schools of psychotherapy has ever tried to explain the healing benefits of forgiveness.

In the field of psychology, works dealing with the therapeutic value of forgiveness are surprisingly rare. To my knowledge, none of the major schools of psychotherapy has ever tried to explain the healing benefits of forgiveness. In fact, they have not even tried to make room for forgiveness in their ideas of personality (Shontz and Rosenak 1988: 23, 29). This gap very likely results from a tendency to reduce forgiveness to a purely religious phenomenon. If so, it is a serious mistake. As we have seen, forgiveness touches upon all aspects of the human person, the biological and psychological as much as the spiritual.

Furthermore, forgiveness is a very pertinent issue these days. There is more and more interest in it as one of the important factors in physical, psychological and spiritual health. Theologians, psychologists, doctors and healers are just starting to discover its therapeutic value. Why the sudden interest? Maybe because, little by little, we are starting to move away from a notion of forgiveness as something magical or that can be produced on command. Will alone does not produce forgiveness. Forgiveness follows the laws of human development and conforms to an individual's stages of maturation. Far from resulting from a burst of determination, forgiveness arises from a process that involves all of a person's faculties and follows a journey of many steps.

The number of steps differs from author to author. Based on my personal and clinical experience and research, I have concluded that twelve steps are necessary for true forgiveness. Why twelve? Because of how people learn. In dividing the challenges of forgiving into a series of steps, I have tried to develop an approach that makes forgiveness readily accessible to the greatest number of people. Clearly forgiveness is not a mechanism that we can pull apart however we wish. This is why I have broken down forgiveness into tasks that seem do-able. While I am not trying to invent a foolproof recipe for forgiveness, I am convinced that, although there may seem to be a lot of them, these markers on the always uncertain path of forgiveness are useful.

Let's look at how these steps in the process of forgiveness are arranged. We began with the firm decision to not seek revenge, on the one hand, and, on the other, to insist that the offender cease their offences. That is the first step. The next three steps deal with healing the wound: recognizing it, sharing it with someone so we can clearly identify it, and mourning it. The fifth step is to accept our anger and desire for revenge. The sixth step, forgiving ourselves, is a major turning point on the path to forgiveness. After the first six steps, which focus our efforts on taking care of ourselves, we can then try to understand our offender (seventh step). Then, we look for the meaning that this wound may eventually offer to our lives (eighth step).

The next three steps are of a more spiritual nature: we know that we deserve forgiveness and that we are already forgiven; we stop trying to forgive; we open ourselves up to the grace of forgiveness. The twelfth and last step addresses what follows forgiveness: we ask ourselves whether it is better to end this relationship or renew it.

You may decide to move quickly through some steps and to linger over those you find especially challenging.

Here, then, is the list of what we must do to achieve true forgiveness:

1. *Decide to not seek revenge and to put a stop to the offensive actions.*
2. *Recognize our pain and inner poverty.*
3. *Share our pain with someone.*
4. *Clearly identify what has been lost so we can grieve it.*
5. *Accept our anger and desire for revenge.*
6. *Forgive ourselves.*
7. *Start to understand the offender.*
8. *Discover what the pain means in our life.*
9. *Know that we are worthy of forgiveness and are already forgiven.*
10. *Stop trying so hard to forgive.*
11. *Open up to the grace of forgiveness.*
12. *Decide whether to end the relationship or to renew it.*

I have charted this course realizing that each of you will use this map as you see fit during your journey of forgiveness. You may decide to move quickly through some steps and to linger over those you find especially challenging. A journal would help you keep track of your progress.

Each step includes an exercise or a questionnaire that helps you pull your thoughts and feelings together and complete the required task before you move on to the next step. The style of these exercises may sometimes surprise you. They are designed to help you truly experience a process of forgiveness as you move along this path. For this reason, the exercises in this book are designed for listening. I recommend that you tape them so that as you listen to them, they can guide you more easily on the path of forgiveness indicated here.

When my heart will not forgive ...

To avoid any further suffering, my embittered and hardened heart swore it would never love again.

No matter how much I beg it to forgive so that it can heal, it remains cold, silent and inaccessible.

I laid out my shivering heart so the sun could caress it.

With the rain's delicate tenderness I watered it.

With warm presence I nourished it.

I rocked it as I would a feverish and sullen child:
I consoled it with tales of love renewed.

My heart would like to believe me. Timid and frightened, it opens up, but just barely. It wavers between the desire to love again and the need to protect its wounded pride.

Finally, it feels pain and weeps, knowing its shame and humiliation.

Is the path of suffering the only way to forgiveness for ourselves and others?

CHAPTER 8

Step One
Do Not Seek Revenge: Put an End to the Offending Actions

Violence never put an end to violence, only non-violence can.
— UNIVERSAL BUDDHIST PRINCIPLE

The spirit of retaliation keeps re-opening your wound by reminding you of the offence.

At the very outset of your inner pilgrimage to forgiveness, I suggest you make two important decisions: do not seek revenge and stop the offensive actions. You can't engage in the process of forgiveness as long as you want to satisfy your desire for revenge, for you will invest all your energy in being a victim.

DECIDING TO NOT SEEK REVENGE

Let's first deal with revenge, which is an instinctive reaction to an undeserved offence. The thirst for vengeance is a bad guide. Avoid it and you will avoid many complications, for, as the Chinese proverb says, "He who seeks revenge should dig two holes." But there is more: claiming your "pound of human flesh" as compensation for the humiliation you suffered, as Shakespeare's Shylock did in *The Merchant of Venice*, may relieve your inner resentment for a short time, but it will not stop it. On the contrary, revenge will bring on a whole series of disappointments and misfortunes that I have listed below. Before you look at them, I want to point out that this list is not based on moral prohibitions, but on common sense and a wish for your happiness. This is called reality therapy, a form of therapy that takes into account reality and your well-being. So, take time to read and ponder the arguments in favour of avoiding revenge, and then ask yourself: "Given all these reasons, do I really still want revenge?"

Punishing someone for the sheer pleasure of revenge will arouse deep feelings of guilt in you.

• Revenge focuses your attention and energy on the past. There is no space for the present and the future holds no interest.

• The spirit of retaliation keeps re-opening your wound by reminding you of the offence. You cannot enjoy the peace and calm your wound needs to scar over and heal.

• To satisfy your desire for revenge, you will have to imitate your offender, in spite of yourself, and let yourself be dragged into their infernal cycle. Not only will you hurt yourself more, but you will also demean yourself in the process.

• Those who opt for revenge repeatedly engage in offensive activity, which stifles any form of creativity and hinders their personal growth.

• Punishing someone for the sheer pleasure of revenge will arouse deep feelings of guilt in you. You will feel guilty for using another person's suffering to relieve your own humiliation.

• While out of spite you may condemn the person who has hurt you, beware lest what you do to the other eventually comes back to you, and that others may soon repay you in kind.

• Your response, even if you think it justified, will leave you afraid and anxious. You will dread the day when your offender counter-attacks.

• Revenge will fuel your resentment, hostility and anger, all feelings that generate stress. You are no doubt familiar with its harmful effects. By attacking the immune system, it leaves you vulnerable to a whole series of stress-related illnesses.

Such are the consequences of revenge. I hope that they will keep you from choosing this path and encourage you to choose the less costly and more rewarding option of forgiveness.

Using all your energy to stop offensive actions is nothing at all like revenge.

If you have considered all the reasons for not seeking revenge, and still find that you cannot control the impulse to do so, I recommend that you go immediately to the fifth step in this process, where you will learn to control your anger and desire for revenge.

END THE OFFENSIVE ACTIONS

Someone once commented to me: "Isn't asking your enemy to stop their offending actions a veiled form of revenge?" Using all your energy to stop offensive actions is nothing at all like revenge. Rather, you respect yourself without attacking your offender. Still, your request may be worded as a humiliating remark if you do it to attack or try to make the offender feel guilty. This is why it is so important to maintain a revenge-free attitude when trying to stop repeated offences.

As long as the behaviour continues, it is useless to think about forgiveness. How can we forgive, or even consider forgiving, when we are constantly subjected to violence? Forgiving under such circumstances is like giving up our rights and becoming cowards. Gandhi, the great apostle of non-violence, thought no differently when he stated: "If the only choice were between violence and cowardice, I would never hesitate to advocate violence."

Fortunately, there are other options for putting an end to injustice: recourse to the justice system is one. I have known parents who, with the backing of their support group, have found the strength and courage to denounce their own son for drug trafficking. Battered wives have overcome their fear and turned to the legal system for protection from their husband's violence. In both cases, these people were obviously resolved

Forgiveness does not excuse us from having the courage to call an offender to task or turn to the legal system, if necessary.

not to seek revenge, but to put an end to terror and injustice and, eventually, to get help for the offender.

In this respect, it seems significant that the Christ who asked us to forgive our enemies did not forgive the merchants in the Temple before chasing them out. He deemed it right and urgent to first stop them profaning the Temple. I recommended this kind of behaviour to a man who, in the midst of settling property division and child custody issues as part of his divorce, asked how he could forgive his wife. I told him that he first had to carry out the legal process as honestly as possible; then, and only then, could he devote his energy to forgiving his wife.

Let me use a personal experience to develop this point. A while ago I heard from two different sources that one of the members of my religious order, with whom I had always been cordial, was accusing me, in front of my colleagues and behind my back, of extracting excessively high fees from the very institution where he was working. I was hurt and indignant to learn that my reputation had been tarnished by such underhanded remarks. My first reaction was to pay no attention to the slander. Then, remembering that I was teaching others that it is imperative to stop offensive actions, I picked up my pen and wrote: "Father, I hear that you have been talking about my supposedly high fees, and all this behind my back. Is this true or false? If it is false, just throw this letter in the garbage. If it is true, I ask that you stop spreading such ideas about me. If you require further explanation, I am prepared to offer it to you, even if the matter of my salary in no way concerns you." The priest immediately stopped his gossip and I was better able to forget about the whole thing.

As these examples show clearly, forgiveness does not excuse us from having the courage to call an offender to task or turn to the legal system, if necessary. Pope John Paul II forgave Agça, his assassin, but never asked that he be excused from the law.

Forgiveness is impossible as long as you let the offender continue their offensive actions.

Exercise

COMING TO TERMS WITH BEING THE VICTIM

This questionnaire will help you come to terms with a situation where you are the victim. I know I don't have to remind you that forgiveness is impossible as long as you let the offender continue their offensive actions.

What do you do in a situation in which you are the victim of another individual's actions?

- *You try to forget.*
- *You let the situation deteriorate.*
- *You tell yourself that nothing can be done.*
- *You fear how the offender would react if you asked that they stop their destructive behaviour.*
- *You let your resentment grow.*
- *You wait for the right moment to seek revenge.*
- *You are afraid that you'll "lose it" or do something totally out of proportion to the offence.*

How can you intervene effectively without resorting to revenge?

With whom could you discuss the situation to reduce your fear and hostility and find the most appropriate and effective means of dealing with the situation?

How do you want to confront your offender?

CHAPTER 9

Step Two
Recognize Your Pain and Poverty

The truth shall set you free. — St. John

No one who continues to deny that they have been hurt and that their inner poverty has been laid bare will be able to forgive.

A very experienced psychotherapist once told me: "I have come to believe that the origin of most neuroses is a refusal to suffer." Once we have been hurt, we run the risk of never being able to offer real forgiveness unless we recognize and admit to ourselves our suffering. In the end, the forgiveness we think we granted becomes nothing more than a form of defence against suffering.

No one who continues to deny that they have been hurt and that their inner poverty has been laid bare will be able to forgive. Therefore, one of your first tasks will be to relive the offence. This time, however, you will do so with greater self-confidence, especially if you ask someone to accompany you on this inner quest. You will learn to accept the suffering the offence caused, to tend to it and transform it to your advantage. The offence is a bit like a sliver in your finger: you can't remove it by ripping it out — you have to push it in deeper to expose its tip and then remove it.

The centering exercise that I propose at the end of this chapter will teach you to look at yourself so that you can move through this emotional phase of forgiveness. But first, it is important that you become aware of the defence mechanisms we use to protect ourselves from suffering.

When suffering becomes unbearable, the psyche tries to diminish its impact in various ways.

DEFENCE MECHANISMS

The human psyche is well organized to defend itself against too much suffering. When suffering becomes unbearable, the psyche tries to diminish its impact in various ways. Biologically, it mobilizes the body's natural pain-killing hormones. Psychologically, defence or resistance mechanisms act as fuses that prevent excessive currents from overloading the electrical circuit. More precisely, these mechanisms paralyze the destructive effects of overwhelming feelings so that the whole organism can survive.

Some authors in the field of psychology do not seem to appreciate just how useful these defence mechanisms are. They think such mechanisms should be eliminated as soon as possible, forgetting that these physiological and psychological defences possess an innate wisdom. They allow wounded people to survive and pursue their daily activities without collapsing completely. Thanks to these defence mechanisms the wounded soldier finds the strength to run long distances to seek help; a mother grief-stricken by her husband's death learns to stifle her pain so that she can keep caring for her children; a businessman threatened with imminent bankruptcy finds the courage to pursue his daily routine without allowing himself to be beaten. Like a police officer who wears a bullet-proof vest in the safety of his or her own home, however, these defence mechanisms will be useless or even harmful if they continue to protect people once the danger is past.

This psychological resistance falls into two main categories: cognitive resistance and emotional resistance. By examining them more closely, we will be able to identify them more readily.

Burying our heads in the sand no doubt lessens the pain and disappointment, but it also sets the stage for bitter awakenings later.

COGNITIVE RESISTANCE

Since I already addressed it in Chapter 3, here I will touch only briefly on the topic of cognitive resistance: denying the offence or trying to minimize its impact. This type of resistance may take several forms. First, there is forgetting: some people claim that forgetting the offence or its impact would be the ideal act of forgiving. Then there are the excuses: people try to invent all sorts of false excuses to relieve the offenders of responsibility. Finally, a similar trap consists of erasing a conflict with a quick and superficial gesture of forgiveness.

There are many ways to justify cognitive resistance. They are all the more compelling when someone close to us has betrayed us or committed a serious injustice against us, an offence so painful and threatening that we prefer to ignore it. Thus, despite all the signs, a husband refuses to accept evidence that his wife has been unfaithful or a boss that a seemingly devoted employee is stealing; even if she detects all the behaviours of a drug user, a mother cannot believe that her son is doing drugs. Burying our heads in the sand no doubt lessens the pain and disappointment, but it also sets the stage for bitter awakenings later.

Sometimes, cognitive resistance makes someone totally forget an event. As with the social worker whose story I told you in Chapter 5, the event still continues to harm behaviour, even years later. His subconscious had completely buried and forgotten the painful event at the hospital as well as his childhood decision never to trust men again. He could not have gone through a process of forgiveness had he not been able to unearth the source of the frustration and shame that had led him to never again trust his male superiors.

There is a close relationship between shame and emotional resistance and, consequently, forgiveness.

EMOTIONAL RESISTANCE

While recent research into alcohol and drug dependency has revealed that unresolved shame plays an important role in emotional resistance, we are barely starting to explore shame and the defence mechanisms that serve to camouflage it. Until now, more often than not the feeling of shame was confused with guilt. But they are not interchangeable. They have neither the same origin nor the same function. The feeling of guilt comes from an awareness that we have broken a law or violated a moral principle that represents a personal or social ideal that we support. Shame is the feeling that the inner self is laid bare, exposed for all to see. Shame makes us see how vulnerable, powerless, incompetent, inadequate and dependent we are. A person struggling with feelings of guilt says: "I have done wrong, I am guilty and I feel guilty," whereas the person who feels shame says: "I am bad and worthless. I am so scared of being rejected." The feeling of guilt, therefore, results from an awareness that we have not reached our ideal, while the feeling of shame emerges from a sharp consciousness of the deficiencies and vulnerability of our inmost self. People who are ashamed feel that their weaknesses are exposed for everyone to see; they always feel the threat of ridicule and rejection.

Some will ask: "Why insist so much on the relationship between shame and forgiveness?" Because there is a close relationship between shame and emotional resistance and, consequently, forgiveness. The offence produces feelings of humiliation and guilt which are even stronger when the offence is committed by someone we love or respect, or someone on whom we are dependent. Then it exposes our dependence and more or less childish needs. Our disappointment is even more acute when the very person from whom we expected affection and respect humiliates us.

Anger and the desire for revenge often serve to hide our shame.

Wanting to forgive without becoming aware of the humiliation and shame that follow the offence is like walking a path booby-trapped with land-mines that has no exit. No matter how generous it may be, the desire to forgive masks a need to protect ourselves against the shame of "feeling small."

The main challenge that we must face during the emotional phase of forgiveness is to recognize our deep feeling of shame so we can accept it, put it in context, digest it and integrate it. Once befriended in this way, it not only becomes more bearable, but it makes us more aware of the powerlessness and finiteness that all human beings share. But the feeling of shame is not easy to uncover. We must recognize that it hides behind the masks of anger, desire for power, moral superiority, the eternal victim complex and perfectionism.

Anger and the desire for revenge often serve to hide our shame. Instead of befriending shame, the humiliated victim reacts by trying to humiliate the offender in turn. In an attempt to free themselves from this shame, they project it on their aggressor to make them suffer the same fate. Sometimes anger and the need to punish have a boomerang effect on some individuals. Having repressed all their aggression, they turn their anger and their desire for revenge against themselves. Shame then hides behind feelings of anxiety and self-punishing guilt, which make it even harder to detect. In this sense, we could say that people prefer feeling guilty to feeling ashamed and powerless. Sometimes, forgiveness granted in a moment of repressed anger is a subtle form of revenge. This could explain why those who receive such an act of forgiveness feel very uncomfortable: instead of feeling free, they feel confused and often humiliated.

The desire for power is another camouflage for shame.

As contradictory as it may seem, when some people are humiliated, they adopt attitudes of power and superiority to try to avoid feeling the powerlessness that their shame produces. Then they will be inclined to exaggerate their own importance and see others as inferior in knowledge, moral qualities and power. In the language of transactional analysis, these people claim to be "okay" and others seem to be "not okay." They act like know-it-alls because they are afraid to face their inner poverty, the mere thought of which makes them extremely anxious. As a result, their concept of forgiveness becomes tainted and they use it mainly to ensure that they will dominate.

The desire for power is another camouflage for shame. By assuming a false moral superiority, victims, unable to accept humiliation, use forgiveness to humiliate the offender in turn. They seem to be saying: "I'm better than you and I'll prove it by forgiving you." Obviously this form of forgiveness hides a great deal of conceit and contempt towards others.

In contrast to this moral arrogance is the person who has learned to use shame to attract the pity of others. By reversing the strategy, these eternal victims know how to exploit to their advantage the faults of whoever "persecutes" them. They always complain about their persecutors and their misdeeds; they talk about their suffering to anyone who cares to listen, parade the ill-treatment they must endure with barely concealed servility. By the same token, they arouse their listeners' indignation towards their oppressor. Once the long-suffering victims declare that they are prepared to forget the offences that have been inflicted on them, they are merely presenting themselves as worthy of admiration and praise.

We need to first clean up our own emotional universe before we can truly forgive.

Take, for example, the perfectionism that one injured party tried to adopt. As children, perfectionists are often subjected to a lot of shame. In his family, this man had always been threatened with shame as a form of discipline. Perhaps he experienced a lot of shame as a result of the erratic behaviour of an alcoholic parent. As a child, he may have sworn never to be found at fault so he would never again be ashamed. To do this, he had to try to become flawless in everything and everywhere. As a model of virtue, he had to make himself forgive. Forgiveness helped him protect the fragile facade that he believed was indestructible.

These are some of the psychological traps that may interfere with the healing of the human heart in the process of forgiveness. They often tend to camouflage the feelings of humiliation and shame that lurk behind false forgiving. Thus they prevent forgiveness from becoming a liberating and fulfilling act. This is why we need to first clean up our own emotional universe before we can truly forgive.

Tensions, stiffness, pain, even certain physical illnesses reflect unexpressed suffering.

Exercise

RECOGNIZING YOUR WOUNDEDNESS AND POVERTY

This exercise is designed to eliminate all resistance to useless and even harmful suffering and shame. It will help you come to terms with your truth and start preparing for the next stage, sharing with another person.

As we have just seen, the human psyche does not easily allow painful experiences to emerge into full consciousness. It protects itself against suffering and, especially, against shame. This exercise, then, does not try to break down your psychological resistance or even get rid of it, but first helps you to become aware of it, then accept it and let it melt away on its own.

The best way to do this is to go back to where these experiences have hidden themselves: in our bodies. Our bodies record everything and retain an accurate memory of the offence and its physical and psychological consequences. Tensions, stiffness, pain, even certain physical illnesses reflect unexpressed suffering. They indicate that a wound needs healing.

If you are ready to start the exercise, concentrate on creating a peaceful atmosphere around you. Plan to be undisturbed for about twenty minutes. Find a comfortable position. Wear loose-fitting clothes.

Take a few minutes to go inside yourself.

If you are a believer, place yourself in the presence of your God or any other spiritual resource that is significant to you. This will give you more courage to get in touch with your pain and your poverty.

Start by calling to mind the experience of the offence. Be sure to pay attention to your body's reactions. If you can't remember the experience, just become aware of your tension, your stiffness and even your physical symptoms. Pay special attention to what is going on around your heart muscle.

If several physical reactions occur at the same time, accept them all for a few minutes. Then, force yourself to focus on the reaction that seems most important or most significant.

Remain aware of your tension or pain without trying to change them or justify them. Welcome this suffering part of yourself very gently and kindly.

Just as gently, ask your tension: "What are you hiding? What's happening? I'm ready to listen to you." You can also speak directly to your heart: "What do you remember about the offence that is keeping you from living fully?"

Stay in touch with your tension and your pain. Prepare to receive what comes without censoring anything. Let images, words and feelings come to the surface without trying to interpret, change or eliminate them.

You can also repeat in your own words the messages that stream forth in the form of images, words or sensations. Ask this part of yourself: "Did I understand properly this memory or this image that you are bringing me? Are these the words you're telling me? Does this feeling come from you or somewhere else?" This is how you show your pure and simple acceptance of what is coming to you, without judging, explaining or wanting to change yourself.

If nothing comes to mind, patiently keep in touch with your body. If you get impatient, concentrate on your impatience and let it speak to you.

When you're satisfied with what you have learned, thank this suffering part of yourself for its willingness to communicate with you. Promise to meet it again and prepare to take your leave of it.

Congratulations on having the courage to connect with the wounded part of yourself and face your inner poverty. It would be good to repeat the exercise. Rarely does the subconscious reveal itself all at once. Rather, it lets you digest its contents bit by bit. To close, it would be good for you to note in your journal everything you've learned about yourself during this exercise.

CHAPTER 10

Step Three
Share Your Pain with Someone

If I am listened to, simply listened to, I have all the
space to myself, and yet, there is someone there. — MAURICE BELLET

When you tell your story to someone who agrees to play the part of "the Ear," you are no longer alone.

There are many possible reactions to a put-down, a betrayal or an attack. Between the defensive reaction of the people who isolate themselves and that of those long-suffering souls who play the martyr lies a healthier option that has more potential for healing: sharing your pain with someone who knows how to listen to you without judging, moralizing, overwhelming you with advice, or minimizing your difficulties, however disturbing they may be. The success of the emotional phase of forgiveness will depend in large part on your opening up honestly to an attentive listener.

WHY SHARE YOUR WOUNDED INNER SELF?
One of the most unbearable aspects of pain is feeling that you are carrying this burden all alone. When you tell your story to someone who agrees to play the part of "the Ear," you are no longer alone. Someone else shares not only your secret, but also the burden of your suffering.

In addition, telling someone about yourself lets you relive the painful event more calmly. This will help you become aware of the emotions that are just below the surface of your being. The past comes alive and is made present. You relive the painful experience, but this time in a safer context. Thanks to the trust you place in your confidant, you will become more confident. Your perception of the offence changes: you will find it seems less threatening and more bearable.

Their unconditional acceptance will slowly start to rub off on you.

No doubt you already know that it is easier to find a solution to another person's problem than to your own. This is what will happen when you confide in someone who serves as a mirror or sounding board. As you begin to distance yourself from your difficulties and see them in a broader perspective, you will be better disposed to deal with them.

There is a final advantage to conversation with an empathetic person: their unconditional acceptance will slowly start to rub off on you. Their acceptance will better dispose you to accept yourself compassionately. I assure you that this self-acceptance will bring you inner peace and calm.

The beneficial effects of sharing one's state of mind with a confidant are incontestable. Can we expect the same from sharing with the person who has injured us?

SHARING WITH THE OFFENDER

Clinical psychologist James Sullivan states in *Journey to Freedom* (1987: 149) that the success of "emotional forgiveness" depends on three essential conditions: that the offender recognize their fault, express their regret and decide to never repeat the offence again. I once encountered a situation where all three conditions existed at once. It was a rather banal incident, but one that could have degenerated into a permanently simmering conflict. I was watching the news on television one evening with about ten members of my religious community. One of them found an empty juice bottle beside a chair. Certain that I was responsible for this act of negligence, he grabbed the bottle, thrust it in my direction and, in an accusatory tone, said to me: "Whose bottle is this?" I don't need to add that the effect of his actions was increased tenfold by the presence of witnesses; I did not fail to notice the barely concealed grins of my

"A wrong confessed is half forgiven."

colleagues. It seemed as if they were waiting for nothing more than this incident to confirm what they already believed: I was absent-minded.

Without uttering a word I took the bottle, but I was seething with anger. Until I went to bed, I indulged in fantasies of revenge, each more elaborate than the previous one. At morning meditation, I was surprised at how much importance the previous evening's confrontation had taken on for me. As I searched for the reason behind such turmoil, I discovered some old wounds that had opened up and decided, on the spot, to put away any thought of revenge and to meet with the confrere who had made the accusation.

I waited for just the right moment when I was alone with him. I told him how angry and humiliated his words had made me feel. To my great surprise, my confrere humbly apologized, blaming his behaviour on his tremendous exhaustion. Then, for the next hour, he told me about his own problems. My openness had invited his own, which created a new intimacy between us.

Then I could better understand the old adage: "A wrong confessed is half forgiven." I felt all my resentment melt away as I listened to his admission and his apology. Without even thinking of it, I had forgiven him.

I should also mention that before I confronted my confrere, I had prepared myself thoroughly: I prayed; I took care to weigh my words carefully; from the outset, I delivered my message to him using the non-confrontational "I." In doing so, I wanted to avoid any hurtful counter-accusations. I ended up delivering my emotional reaction in a simple, non-confrontational way. In addition, I was determined to hear him out and pursue the dialogue with him until we had cleared up the situation together.

It gets complicated when offenders refuse to acknowledge what they have done or are absent, unreachable, unknown or dead.

WHEN SHARING WITH THE OFFENDER IS IMPOSSIBLE

But what happens if the person who committed the offence does not want to talk or hear about it, as was the case with a young woman who was an incest victim? Following a long period of therapy, she felt the need to tell her father about the disastrous consequences of the sexual abuse to which he had subjected her. She felt she was racing against time, since her father had terminal cancer. Her father had always avoided the subject. With no possibility of dialogue with him, she felt she could not forgive him.

I advised her to use the heart's silent language to ease her pain and hostility, and eventually to forgive him. She agreed. During periods of silence at his bedside, she forged a deep rapport with him by synchronizing her breathing with his; then she told him in her heart about all that she had suffered because of the incest. After several sessions where she let her heart speak, she felt forgiveness rise in her and, as a result, felt a deep sense of relief. Strangely, her father appeared much calmer to her.

It gets complicated when offenders refuse to acknowledge what they have done or are absent, unreachable, unknown or dead. In such cases, James Sullivan (1987: 149-152) suggests the counsellor play the part of the offender, acknowledge guilt in their name and express their regret and firm resolve. To illustrate his point, he tells the story of a nun who was continuously depressed because her mother had rejected her as a child. Once he recognized that the nun was seeing in him the image of her mother, Sullivan agreed to play the mother's part. He asked for forgiveness for having neglected her as a child. Then he expressed his delight at having found her again and at being able

When you are faced with an unrepentant and stubborn offender, your last recourse is to commend them to God's care.

to learn to love her once again. According to the psychologist, these exchanges were so beneficial that the nun was able to connect with her inner child and allow her to relive and express feelings that had remained frozen inside for all those years. She cried a lot, got angry and finally forgave her mother.

It is not always possible to find a counsellor who can help by playing the part of the offender. In that case, you must resort to substitutes: writing letters without mailing them or having a conversation with a chair while imagining the offender seated in it.

When you are faced with an unrepentant and stubborn offender, your last recourse is to commend them to God's care, as the Jewish saying recommends: "If your offender does not want to reform, hand him over to divine justice." This is precisely what the director of a large institution did. When he learned that I was planning to write about forgiveness, he told me his story, no doubt with the unstated intention of having me share it with my readers. As the victim of dishonest dealings by two of his colleagues, he lost a high administrative position; his career was shattered. He then went through a deep depression from which he managed to emerge thanks to a piece of advice he found in the works of Michael Murphy on the topic of forgiveness. Several times a day, he repeated the following prayer: "Dear God, powerless as I am, I give my colleagues (at this point he mentioned their names) to your infinite mercy so that you may convert to good the injustice they did to me, and may your will be done." He assured me that within three months of this program of invocation, he no longer felt any trace of anger or resentment. Upon meeting his former detractors at a conference, he surprised himself by shaking hands with them without a moment's hesitation.

Exercise
SHARING YOUR WOUND

From all the means of sharing recommended in this chapter, choose the one that best suits your own process of forgiveness.

Speak to your offender face to face, after carefully preparing yourself as follows:

- *decide to impart your feelings to him or her through "I" messages*

- *listen to his or her version of the story*

- *take the exchange as far as you can.*

Find someone who knows how to listen without judging.

Practise the "language of the heart" in difficult situations.

Entrust your offender to God through prayer.

CHAPTER II

Step Four
Identify Your Loss Properly So You Can Grieve It

I suffered an offence but I was not offended deep within my being.

— ANONYMOUS

If you do not grieve what you lost, you will not really know how to forgive.

On the long journey to forgiveness, you started by recognizing the damage the offence caused you and you talked about it with an empathetic person. This clarified your situation and lightened your burden. Now you are well on the way to healing. During this fourth step I suggest you make a detailed inventory of the losses you suffered because of this offence; the emerging awareness will help you grieve them. If you do not grieve what you lost, you will not really know how to forgive.

IDENTIFY YOUR LOSS PROPERLY
A personal experience helped me to understand how important it is to carefully identify a wound before it can be healed. One day, I received a letter from a young man who wanted to enroll at the university where I was teaching. He asked me to send him some information on the program I was in charge of, but neglected to give me his address. Since he was already registered in another department of the same university, I suppose he thought that this was not necessary. So, thinking it the sensible thing to do, I went to get the information from the secretary of that department. But the secretary did not take to it kindly when I put the request to her and, once she had given me the third degree, squarely refused to give me the information. Worse still, she accused me of raiding another academic unit and threw me out of her office. Stunned, I didn't

We are hurt more by our interpretation of an unpleasant event than by the event itself.

realize what was happening to me, and found myself over-whelmed by indignation. So I sat down and wrote to the president asking that he arrange to have this rude employee fired. I was just finishing writing my vitriolic letter when one of my colleagues walked into my office. I told him about my ordeal. He heard me out and then asked me pointedly: "You seem pretty angry. What sensitive spot did she hit in you?" At first, I found his question inappropriate and rude. Upon reflection, however, I realized two things: the secretary had questioned my professional honesty and had also opened up an old wound I had thought forgotten. This new awareness had an unexpected effect on me: to my great surprise, my anger and resentment faded away to the point where I no longer felt the need to send my letter to the president.

What could cause such a sudden change? This is how I explain it. When the unfortunate incident happened, I felt that my whole being had been called into question. Later, I understood that the secretary had questioned only part of me: my professional honesty. Discovering this let me see my pain in a new light. First, it no longer seemed so huge. Second, I realized that I was less disturbed by the recent unpleasant episode with the secretary than by the painful situation I had not yet resolved.

J. Trotter's article (1987: 31-39) on the research findings of the psychologist Martin Saligman shed more light on what had happened. Saligman maintains that we are hurt more by our interpretation of an unpleasant event than by the event itself. He believes that people who consider themselves as the total, unique and permanent cause of an unfortunate event are condemned both to underestimate themselves and to be incapable of reacting. To better grasp the meaning of the

*Settling for being
a victim saps
your energy.*

terms "total, unique and permanent," we only have to listen to the inner dialogue people will wage against themselves in an effort to understand their disappointments. They tend to blame themselves totally and utterly, as if they were suffering from some congenital defect. "I've always been clumsy and incompetent," they say, rather than encouraging themselves by saying instead: "I've made a mistake, but it can be corrected." Next, they take full responsibility for the mistake. "It's all my fault," they say, rather than realizing that they are not solely responsible for the situation and that other parties are involved. Finally, they see themselves as perpetual victims of destiny. "It never happens to anyone else but me," they complain, instead of telling themselves: "This is the result of a passing set of circumstances."

STOP BLAMING YOURSELF

Settling for being a victim saps your energy. Beating yourself up is always a bad response that will keep you from moving ahead on the journey to forgiveness. To get out of the slump, I suggest you do the following exercises:

1. Ask yourself which part of you was hurt. What did you lose? What precious aspect of you was attacked or mistreated? Which expectations or dreams were suddenly destroyed?

These may have been damaged: self-esteem, reputation, self-confidence, integrity, faith in others, devotion to those who are close to you, ideals, dreams of happiness, material goods, health, beauty, social image, expectations of authority, the need to be able to trust someone with your secrets, admiration for those you love, etc.

You are not the only one responsible for the painful event or offence.

Once you have identified and named your loss, become aware that it is not your whole being that was offended, but only part of yourself. It would be helpful to repeat: "It is not my whole being that was hurt, it was (for instance) my reputation that was damaged." Some time ago, I heard the televised testimony of a woman who had been raped. She said: "I was raped but not violated." In other words, she was saying: "The heart of my being has remained healthy and whole in spite of the rape and I have not lost the capacity to heal myself."

I'd also like to draw your attention to how the way you talk about what happened to you changes your perception of the event. There is a huge difference in the perception of the situation, depending on whether you say, "I am handicapped" or "I have a handicap." When someone says: "I have a wound," it implies a distance between my whole being and the wound, a distance that lets me react and heal myself. On the other hand, when I state: "I am wounded," I identify my whole being with the wound and thus make myself unable to react.

2. Remember that you are not the only one responsible for the painful event or offence. I told the participants in a conference I was giving for separated and divorced people that they were not solely responsible for their marital breakdown. Their ex-spouse, their parents, society, etc., also shared the responsibility. One participant burst into tears when she heard this. When I asked her what was happening, she said that, for the first time, she realized that she was not the horrible person solely responsible for the breakdown of her marriage.

3. Finally, it is important to convince yourself completely that an error is not irreparable. You are not condemned to

The hardest wounds to recognize and identify are those which go back to the distant past of our childhood.

reliving it endlessly or to suffering its consequences. If you see yourself as constantly pursued by misfortune or bad luck, you will inevitably program yourself for new failures.

So, instead of tormenting yourself over a new failure, try to discover what you can learn from it. So many failures have been the seeds of enriching experiences, new beginnings and success in life. One more positive aspect of your mistakes: they make you much more tolerant towards others.

HEALING CHILDHOOD WOUNDS

The hardest wounds to recognize and identify are those which go back to the distant past of our childhood. We no longer remember either the wounds or what caused them. All that remains are the rigid behaviours and defensive reactions that point to old traumas that are stirred up by the slightest offence.

We continue to feel these childhood misfortunes at an unconscious level many years later. I have often met people who, despite all their best intentions, claim they cannot forgive the smallest thing. Their inability to forgive humiliates them and often makes them feel very guilty. A young woman was telling me about her inability to forgive her father-in-law. His big mistake was that he had stayed with his daughter-in-law for two days even though he had only been invited for a family dinner. At the mere thought of forgiving him, she would come up against strong inner resistance. She ended up berating herself for exaggerating the mistake: "It's a non-issue, I should stop resenting him for it." In total despair, she came to see me. I asked her to define as precisely as possible the nature of the injury. She answered: "I feel like I'm insignificant to him because he just ignored the message of my invitation." Then I suggested that she hold onto that feeling

103

Unexplained blocking during the process of forgiveness very often originates with an old wound.

of being "insignificant" and go back, in her mind, into her past, and allow anything that spontaneously associated with that feeling to surface. Moved to tears, she told me that when she was a child of eight, her mother had promised for a whole year to bring her to Midnight Mass. But when she woke up on Christmas Eve morning, her mother told her that she was still too young to attend Midnight Mass. This childhood disappointment, which she had completely forgotten, echoed across the decades, blocking her desire to forgive her father-in-law. Only when she had uncovered the origin of the feeling of being "insignificant" was she able to forgive, first her mother, and then her father-in-law.

Exercise
HEALING A CHILDHOOD WOUND

My experience as a psychotherapist has taught me that unexplained blocking during the process of forgiveness very often originates with an old wound that is still very alive in the unconscious. This is why I propose meditating on the obstacle itself.

Settle into a comfortable position. Find someplace where you can get away from distractions for about twenty minutes.

Take time to enter within yourself as you did during the other meditation exercises.

Put yourself back into the situation created by the current offence and let yourself relive what happened to you. Give yourself time to clearly identify and name what hurts.

Stay in touch with the emotions you feel rising up in you.

Then, starting from the emotions you currently identify, follow them back into your past as if you were turning the pages of a souvenir album one by one. Still guided by the same emotion(s), let the images, memories and words associated with the various stages of your past life surface.

Once you have reached the most distant memory, take a few minutes to look at the same scene again and relive it. How old are you? Who is with you? What is happening? How are you reacting? What decision are you making as a result of this painful event?

See the child that you were. What are you wearing? Where are you? How would you describe this child? Observe what this child is experiencing just as if he or she were right in front of you.

Now, using all your experience as an adult, all your competence, and all your knowledge of child psychology, start to talk to the child. Reassure the child, asking forgiveness for having forgotten this precious being for so long.

Once you are certain that you have won over your child and that the child agrees to let you get close, stand up, take the child in your arms, sit her on your lap, and hug her very tight by crossing your arms over your chest.

Take time to feel your child's presence, let your child settle down and help this precious being heal. If you think the child is ready, you can suggest that he or she start to forgive the offender. If you feel resistance, don't force it. Just keep holding and comforting your child. You know your child's generosity. Trust that when your child is ready, he or she will forgive.

Before you take leave of your child, reassure him/her by indicating that you are not abandoning him/her, that you will be back to talk to and care for him or her.

Congratulations! You have just taken a giant step in the journey to healing and to "emotional forgiveness." In the next chapter, we will see how to handle your anger and your desire for revenge.

CHAPTER 12

Step Five
Accept Anger and the Desire for Revenge

You have to be a psychotherapist to know how much
repressed aggression lies behind false forgiveness.

— PAUL TOURNIER

To my mind, love is destroyed not by anger, but by indifference and the fear of opening up.

For some people, the word "anger" often evokes scenes of extreme violence. As a result, they develop a great fear of experiencing this emotion. Some spiritual people have a very hard time seeing in anger and the desire for revenge anything akin to a healthy psychological reality. Because of a crippled concept of love, they feel that any tendency towards aggression should be repressed. Here is the story of a confrontation I had with the chaplain of a group for couples. He attended a session on communication I was holding for a few couples. I explained how life as a couple brings its share of frustrations along with its joys. In my opinion, the build-up of frustrations following on the heels of minor misunderstandings and the subsequent feelings of aggravation constitute one of the major obstacles to good communication between two people. This is why I advised the couples to not let their small angers fester deep inside but to express them in the most constructive way possible. To my mind, love is destroyed not by anger, but by indifference and the fear of opening up. At that moment, I saw the chaplain leap to his feet. He shouted at me: "Father, you should know that anger is one of the seven deadly sins!" He stormed out on the spot, slamming the door behind him.

Obviously, we did not share the same definition of anger. I was using this word to describe the state of inner irritability caused by some annoyance, insult or injustice. He, on the

Anger motivates us to seek out authenticity and try to remove obstacles to loving others.

other hand, gave it a meaning of hatred and resentment, feelings that are intended to hurt or even destroy the other person.

Preachers, spiritual directors and New Age advocates often see forgiveness and anger as opposites. They think that to be able to forgive, we must first stifle all anger and chase away all thought of revenge. In essence, they are encouraging repression of all so-called negative feelings. This approach leads nowhere, for, just as granting forgiveness will be impossible if we have not first recognized and embraced our shame, it will be just as impossible if we repress anger and the desire for revenge. We lie to ourselves and turn forgiveness into some kind of social party trick when we do not recognize and accept anger and the desire for revenge just because we say we want to forgive.

But we must be careful. My point here is not to encourage and feed resentment. Far too often, we confuse the spontaneous emotion of anger with resentment. We must distinguish the fleeting emotion of anger and desire for revenge from the deliberate and sustained feeling of hatred or resentment. Although anger is a violent reaction of the soul, despite appearances it contains some positive aspects. As a normal reaction to injustice, anger motivates us to seek out authenticity and try to remove obstacles to loving others. Resentment, on the other hand, roots itself in the human heart like a cancer. It hides an unhearing and obstinate anger that is relieved only when the offender has been punished or humiliated. It may take several forms: sarcasm, lasting hatred, contempt, calculated hostility, blaming and passive aggression that kill any possible hope for joy in a relationship. As long as we refuse to recognize our anger and draw from it all the possible benefits, there is a danger that it will fester inside and turn into resentment and hatred.

Repressed anger may shift onto innocent targets, whether objects, animals or people.

THE DESTRUCTIVE EFFECTS OF REPRESSED ANGER

Repressing anger is like sinking into a swamp with no hope of getting out. When we repress emotions because society deems them unacceptable, we can expect that sooner or later they will re-emerge in some deviant form. It is impossible to repress emotional energy; it always manages to express itself in an artificial and deceptive way. Transactional analysis calls these emotional deviations "counterfeit feelings." Let us examine more closely these "counterfeit feelings" that find their roots in the unhealthy repression of aggressivity.

Repressed anger may shift onto innocent targets, whether objects, animals or people. Who has never seen someone kick an object or even an animal to relieve some pent-up anger? Similar reactions towards people are not uncommon. With some justification, it has been claimed that the husband who beats his wife is desperately trying to free himself from the image of his mother. I have also seen a child go out and punch his younger brother after being scolded by his mother.

An uncontrollable urge for violence often arises from the accumulation of repressed small angers. One of my clients, who always wore a fixed smile, came to see me about learning to control his periodic bouts of verbal violence. His boss was threatening to fire him and his wife was threatening divorce. I refused to help him tackle his anger, for I did not want to fail as had his spiritual director, who had tried everything to keep him from getting angry. Instead, I decided to help him befriend his anger. I asked him not to stifle it, but to let it rise, recognize it through the typical tensions in his body, accept it and find acceptable outlets for it, such as sports, chopping wood on his acreage and other forms of vigorous exercise.

People who have not become aware of their own anger are inclined to pass it on to others.

One of the most common effects of repressing anger is the tendency to project it onto others. People who have not become aware of their own anger are inclined to pass it on to others. When threatened by the masks of their own anger, they attribute it to other people. The following example illustrates what I mean. A well-educated woman who had strong spiritual beliefs wrote me to express her torment over her son's suicide. She told me that she had very quickly forgiven him for the pain and distress it had caused her. However, she could not believe that God would forgive her son such a terrible act. I thought that she was not able to handle her anger towards her son, so she projected it onto God. I was convinced this was the case when her torment and her doubts continued to plague her despite her pastor's efforts to reassure her of God's goodness and mercy.

I replied: "Madam, not for one moment did I ever doubt that you sincerely wanted to forgive your son. But I am surprised by how little time you gave to healing your pain before granting your forgiveness. Do you believe you had worked through enough of your grief and experienced enough healing from this devastating blow to really be able to think about forgiving him? My experience with people in mourning following a suicide of someone they love leads me to believe that it takes a lot of time for anger and guilt to work their way to the surface so they can be transformed. Right now the most important thing you can do is listen to your feelings. That will help you accept those which have not yet had a chance to surface." Some time later, I received a letter in which she told me that I had been right and that she had found herself a good counsellor who was helping her deal with her feelings of guilt and anger.

Repressed anger can wear many other masks: blaming, nagging, icy cynicism, accusing hostility or sulking.

Sometimes people turn repressed anger against themselves. This happens with people who can't allow themselves even the slightest hint of anger, and feel guilty as soon as they detect such feelings in themselves. Then they blame themselves, punish themselves, or fall into a deep depression, as did the social worker who attended one of my seminars on grieving. One of her clients, a young man she had become very fond of, had committed suicide. She reproached herself bitterly for having been away the day he had phoned her asking for help. Ever since, she had been haunted by the notion that she was largely responsible for this suicide. She blamed herself for having toyed with the idea that maybe suicide would have been a solution to his many problems. After listening to her anxiety, I suggested she picture her young client sitting in front of her and repeat to him: "I feel guilty for your death." Then, I suggested she replace that statement with this one: "I am angry at you for having chosen death in spite of all the help I gave you." After a great deal of hesitation, she decided to share her disappointment and anger with him. Her feelings of disappointment and anger got stronger and stronger as she expressed them. Finally, recognizing how impossible it would have been for her to prevent her client's suicide, she burst into tears. She had come to accept her limitations. At that point she started to forgive herself for thinking that she was strong enough to save him in spite of himself.

Repressed anger can wear many other masks: blaming, nagging, icy cynicism, accusing hostility or sulking. All these masks of anger fall into the category of "counterfeit feelings," which are typically never-ending. In contrast, authentic feelings are over as soon as they are expressed. This is the normal outcome of a successful catharsis, or release of feeling. But

Unrecognized anger may cause several psychosomatic illnesses.

with counterfeit feelings it is a whole different story. They poison the person's emotional life without ever being properly expressed. The only way out of this emotional quagmire is to get back in touch with the repressed anger and express it properly.

Because it drains so much energy and creates so much stress, unrecognized anger may cause several psychosomatic illnesses. It produces unhealthy stress that causes a wide variety of physical ailments. In *Healing Life's Hurts* (1987: 135-136), the Linn brothers report the results of research in this area by Dr. Floyd Ring, who studied various illnesses caused by failing to control anger or by expressing it inappropriately. On the one hand, he maintains that excessive displays of anger, be they physical or verbal, often produce the following illnesses: heart attacks, degenerative arthritis and peptic ulcers. On the other hand, people who repress their fear and their anger are subject to skin diseases, rheumatoid arthritis and ulcerative colitis. Finally, people who never dare to express their anger or their fear because of the excessive amount of self-control they exercise, even though they may not be aware of it, run the risk of asthma, diabetes, high blood pressure and migraines. This list may appear rather bleak, but it can be argued that systematic repression of anger provokes such pathological and neurotic conditions that the patient can no longer find the energy to walk the path of forgiveness.

I would like to end this section with a few remarks on how to deal with fantasies of revenge. I have met people who tried to rid themselves of their vengeful thoughts by fighting them head-on. They were wasting their energy. The more they tried to get rid of them, the more they resurfaced in an

Anger, the soul's fierce and aggressive energy, is not harmful in itself.

obsessive manner. The following exercise will help you see this: try *not* to think of the colour "red." It's impossible, right, since in order to imagine non-red, you first have to think of red. In fact, the imagination cannot conceive of non-red. It's the same thing with ideas of revenge. The harder you try to get rid of them, the more insistently they will impose themselves on your imagination. You may as well just calmly let them come to you and unfold, like a movie. Once you do this, and accept them, these fantasies will begin to seem rather futile. All that will remain will be for you to decide whether or not you want to follow up on them.

THE BENEFITS OF ANGER

Anger, the soul's fierce and aggressive energy, is not harmful in itself. It is triggered by an instinct for physical, psychological or moral self-preservation. Whether it is harmful or beneficial depends on how we use it.

When used properly, anger helps keep relationships between spouses, lovers and friends, parents and children, or bosses and employees operating smoothly. In each case, we must defend our boundaries and values, sometimes vigorously and forcefully. In contrast to what happens when we act as though nothing matters or turn our aggression inwards, anger, properly expressed, implies the desire to re-establish contact. When we assert ourselves, even in anger, we are trying to remove obstacles to communication and love.

Owning our aggression, rather than repressing it, can have other beneficial effects. In essence, it arouses the mental energy we need to confront evil and injustice. Thus it can help us discover values that we hold near and dear and reveal more clearly what we want to be and do. It warns of the danger of allowing another to abuse us or invade our personal space. Anger may make us react to injustices towards a person or a group of people.

PUTTING ANGER TO GOOD USE

If repressing anger and the desire for revenge inevitably lead to an impasse, how can we deal with them? Do we seethe with anger or befriend it? The following story offers one answer. Andrew came to me following a painful separation that had left him an emotional wreck. He could barely fulfill his duties as a high school teacher. Constantly depressed, he blamed himself for his wife's departure and for his own angry, verbal outbursts over the past several years, which deeply humiliated him. At times, Andrew could keep his explosive temper in check by sheer willpower, but after a lull in the storm, it took only one insignificant event to make him blow up again. He would apologize profusely, go to confession and listen with great resolve to the reproving and encouraging words of his confessor, but the next outburst of rage would wipe out all of his efforts.

At the outset of therapy, I did not dare broach the subject of anger with him, for fear that he had not yet worked through the grief of his separation. When I thought that he was ready to deal with his repressed anger, I suggested we work on it, but he didn't really seem interested. I still wanted to get the issue of his blow-ups on the table. Although he insisted that his anger was perfectly under control, I was far from convinced. So, one day, I decided to test him. I brought up the question of his wife's infidelities, and his painful and humiliating divorce. He remained impassive. I turned up the heat by reminding him of how he had been the last to know

I suggested that he talk to his anger and tell it that he welcomed it, accepted it and thanked it for being there to protect him.

that his wife was having an affair. Seeing his face slowly turn red and a frown furrow his forehead, I asked him what was happening inside him. At first he denied that he felt anything. I refused to let up, asking him to describe the feelings he was experiencing throughout his body. He admitted that he felt like he had a huge ball in the pit of his stomach. I told him to stay in touch with that ball, but he flatly refused on the pretext that it was wrong to get angry. I reminded him of my ethical and professional skills as a priest and psychologist, and asked him to trust me. Reassured, he concentrated on the ball and began to describe his rising anger and everything he wanted to say and do. Then I suggested that he talk to his anger and tell it that he welcomed it, accepted it and thanked it for being there to protect him. Once more he refused. Again I had to invite him to trust me one more time until he finally agreed to address his anger, greet it as a friend who wanted to protect him and tell it gently that he would not be needing its services right now. He was amazed to discover that the ball in the pit of his stomach was starting to dissolve and spread like a comforting warmth throughout his body.

My client had just reconciled with the angry part of his being that he had been fighting unsuccessfully for so long. Andrew had just emerged from the pattern of alternating repressed and explosive anger that over the years had prevented him from maturing emotionally. Less caught up in his anger, he could now think about achieving real forgiveness.

A few months later, I wanted to check on what effects his reconciliation with his anger had had. He told me the following story: "One day, I was teaching, and I was trying to get my students to listen — to no avail. They were talking louder than I was. I could feel the ball forming in my stomach. I was on

There is no emotion that is negative or shameful in itself.

the verge of one of my outbursts of anger. I heard myself telling them: 'Careful! Right now, I can feel a friend who will know how to make you be quiet is close by – my anger. You know that it's not a pretty sight when it explodes. If you quiet down, it will calm down.' Stunned by my new approach to discipline, my students quieted down. I can swear that I have not had an outburst of anger for four months now. I have learned to recognize and respect it as a friend."

As you probably noticed while you were reading this story, there is no emotion that is negative or shameful in itself. Emotions are made up of positive human energies that need to be recognized, controlled and put to good use. When feared or repressed by the subconscious, they form groups of emotions and images called "complexes" that then take on a life of their own. In Jungian psychology, repressed material forms the "shadow" of the personality which dominates, uncontrollably, as long as people refuse to notice it and try to run away from it. If a person decides to slowly absorb their shadow, as in Andrew's case, what may have seemed to be a destructive handicap will be transformed into a source of energy and personal and social growth.

WHEN PEOPLE ARE AFRAID TO LET GO OF RESENTMENT

Some people who have been hurt refuse to abandon their resentment. They fear that they will betray themselves if they let their resentment and their hatred be transformed. They believe, wrongly, that keeping their resentment alive will preserve their human dignity and keep them from risking further humiliation. Certainly, the desire to have our personal dignity respected is noble, but it is equally clear that nurturing

Like a rocket, resentment can give you an initial boost, but it is short-lived.

resentment leads to a breakdown of the self and ineffective cycles of revenge. There are other ways to maintain our dignity and self-esteem without being eaten up and destroyed by our own animosity.

Others think that resentment and hatred will motivate them to prove their worth and abilities to themselves and others. A participant in one of my conferences insisted that, thanks to her hatred and rancour, she had undertaken and completed her studies. She had wanted to prove to her ex-spouse that she was capable of being financially independent. After congratulating her on her perseverance and academic success, I asked her when she intended to stop acting in relation to her ex-spouse so that she could invest her energies in herself and what she wanted out of her life. Like a rocket, resentment can give you an initial boost, but it is short-lived.

Exercise

RESPECTING ANGER AND THE DESIRE FOR REVENGE

Here is another exercise that will help you get in touch with your anger so you can befriend it and learn what it can do for you. During the exercise, you may encounter emotions other than anger. Don't stop the exercise. Behind anger often lies unconscious suffering and a great deal of shame.

Settle into a comfortable position. Empty your mind of distractions; distance yourself physically as much as possible from anything that could distract you in the next twenty minutes.

Take time to enter into yourself. As you recall the situation in which you were hurt, focus your attention on your body. Without censoring anything, accept all the tensions, stiffness, "balls" and physical discomfort.

Once you have identified an important physical reaction, focus your attention on it respectfully and gently. Don't try to modify, interpret or eliminate it.

Deepen your contact with this physical sensation by breathing into it as if it were a lung that you were filling and emptying.

Remaining centered on your body's reaction, hold your hands at face level. Exhale the air you have just breathed into the sensation, blowing it into your open hands.

As you blow the air into your hands, begin to observe the shape your physical tension takes as it is exhaled. Many people see a cloud of various shapes and colours. At the centre of the cloud, they see a specific image.

Take all the time you need to figure out properly what this tension means. Describe the tension as you see it in the image. Use a name or an expression to describe it.

Whatever emotion this form symbolizes for you, ask it: "What do you want to do for me? What do you want to protect me from? How do you want to help me?" Wait for its reply. Then, repeat its answer back in your own words to show that you have understood its message. Pursue the dialogue with this part of yourself, treating it like a friend.

If you believe in God or some other transcendent spiritual reality, at this point you may want to invoke it and hand your anger, as represented by the symbol, over to it. Ask it to help you transform your anger into a source of personal knowledge, growth and wisdom.

Once you are satisfied with the transformation of your emotional state as represented by the symbol, take this part of yourself back in your hands again, in its new form, and start to inhale it. Let it spread throughout your body.

Now check: how much has your initial physical discomfort changed?

If you wish, celebrate this newly integrated self with a prayer, a song, a dance or just note the experience in your journal.

CHAPTER 13

Step Six
Forgive Yourself

Hating your soul means being unable to forgive yourself,
to exist or to be yourself.
— GEORGES BERNANOS

If you hate yourself,
all your efforts to
forgive others
will be undone.

Forgiving ourselves seems to me to be the turning point in the process of forgiveness. Only when we have forgiven ourselves will the forgiveness we extend to God and others be effective. People who want to forgive but cannot forgive themselves are like swimmers caught in the undertow of the wave: they are constantly being dragged back out to sea, far from shore. If you hate yourself, all your efforts to forgive others will be undone. Even when we have not suffered a specific offence or injury, forgiving ourselves remains one of the great psycho-spiritual aspects of healing. My friend Carol recalled the recommendation of her former psychoanalyst: "The main thing in therapy is to learn to forgive yourself."

When we have been deeply wounded, we no longer hesitate to forgive ourselves. In fact, we are driven to it. When we have been dealt a hard blow, especially by someone dear to us, our inner harmony is shattered. Rival forces are set loose within. Only by humbly forgiving ourselves will we be able to restore our inner peace and harmony, and be open to the possibility of forgiving someone else.

RECOGNIZING SELF-HATRED

Our inner harmony always depends on a fragile and unstable balance. Disappointment, injustice or misfortune awaken discordant inner voices in us. These voices invade almost all the space in our inner world, to the point where no room is left

Only by humbly forgiving ourselves will we be open to the possibility of forgiving someone else.

for forgiveness. Thus wrapped up in ourselves, we are unable to forgive someone else. I noted this during a weekend of healing for separated and divorced people. I asked the participants to describe what prevented them from forgiving. The main obstacle they reported came from their own merciless self-criticism and their inability to forgive. Here are some sample comments:

"I have a hard time forgiving myself because I broke up my family. I didn't think enough before I left; I couldn't tolerate conflicts in our marriage … "

"I should have predicted there'd be problems when I married a man who was so psychologically fragile."

"I blame myself for being so naïve and for trusting him so completely."

"I can't forgive myself for believing that I could change my husband, who's an alcoholic, before I married him."

"I'm angry at myself for believing his lies and enduring his infidelities and his excessive spending for so long."

"The person I find hardest to forgive is me, for being crazy enough and stubborn enough to stick with a marriage that had no future, for having been so materialistic … "

"I find it hard to forgive myself for not having been prepared to forgive."

These comments show to what extent people in deep distress tend to blame themselves. They will not forgive themselves for having left themselves open to such misery, and their distress lays their shortcomings and weaknesses open for all to see. In addition to being humiliated, they feel

Little by little, we have to learn to accept our limitations.

overwhelmed by shame and guilt, which mix in with all the humiliation they've ever experienced.

THE ORIGINS OF A LACK OF SELF-ESTEEM

Three possible sources for lack of self-esteem have been identified: first, disappointment that we could not live up to some dream or ideal. The second is negative messages from parents and other key people in our life. The last is attacks by the shadow side of our personality, which is formed, for the most part, from repressed — and thus undeveloped — human and spiritual potential.

The first source of hostility towards ourselves is the search for absolute happiness and perfection, as if everyone had to be gods or goddesses or, at the very least, princes or princesses. This thirst for the infinite is always at work in us, even though we are flawed, limited creatures. Little by little, we have to learn to accept our limitations, to deal with our feelings of guilt at not being perfect. Being able to actually accept our creaturehood has always been considered a major step on the path to psychological and spiritual health. It is called "humility," the virtue that helps us be clear on who we are. Humility permits us to forgive ourselves, not only for being limited and fallible, but also for having thought that we were all-powerful, without fault, and perfect in all respects.

The negative messages we get from people we see as important in our lives constitute the second source of feelings of guilt and self-hatred. These messages may be non-verbal or verbal. Let's look at the non-verbal negative messages first. Babies pick up a host of non-verbal messages, such as impatience or aggression, in their parents' gestures. Whether these

Lack of self-esteem and even self-hatred will grow as a consequence of verbal put-downs.

result from the parents' tiredness, depression, unconscious rejection of the child, neglect of hygiene, intrusions into the baby's private life, acts of violence, or sexual abuse, babies record it all in their nervous system and memory.

Later, lack of self-esteem and even self-hatred will grow as a consequence of verbal put-downs, such as nasty remarks, spiteful judgments, unfavourable comparisons, ridicule, name-calling, and so on. The accumulation of messages like these can create an inferiority complex that haunts the recipients of such insults. People like this are overwhelmed by their inability to live out the poorly defined ideal that these negative messages have created. Disappointed in themselves, and always seeing themselves as losers, they sink into despair and periodic states of depression, and may even be driven to suicide, the supreme form of refusal to forgive oneself.

The third possible source of feelings of guilt and discomfort towards ourselves comes from the shadow aspect of the personality. The shadow is made up of all the aspects of the self that we have been unable or unwilling to develop because they were seen as unacceptable in our social context. Panic-stricken at the thought that those parts of ourselves that we think unacceptable might be revealed, we bury them in our subconscious. We do this far too often, for instance, with aggression that we are afraid to express. This aggression surfaces at the time of the offence, demanding its rightful place. If, at that moment, it is not welcomed and befriended, it may turn against those who ignore it. Instead of being an ally, it becomes an enemy who attacks with unhealthy self-accusations.

IDENTIFYING WITH THE AGGRESSOR

After an offence, injury or personal attack, a strange phenomenon occurs. In psychology, we call it "identifying with the aggressor." In one sense it is a form of self-preservation, in which we try to escape becoming a victim by putting ourselves in the aggressor's place. By taking on the aggressor's power, the victim has the illusion of preserving a certain dignity or appearance of autonomy. But the problem is that, even once the offence is over, we continue to persecute ourselves. Nearly all the schools of psychology recognize the existence of this defence mechanism that they define by various terms: "superego," "critical parent," "neurotic guilt," "top dog," "superiority complex," and so on.

This part of our being then turns against us, tyrannical and merciless. You know it is at work when you hear certain expressions that make excessive demands on you, and never feel content. Here are a few examples of this inner dialogue: "I have to...," "I must ... ," "I should have ... ." Sometimes, such bitterness comes out in derogatory nicknames and putdowns toward yourself.

Such a dialogue results in two parts of ourselves being in conflict. The two are poles apart. One tends to tyrannize the other through impossible demands, while the other suffers all the accusations and puts itself down for its poor performance or, at other times, rebels. Out of this often subconscious war emerge guilt feelings, diffuse anxiety and depression.

Thus, each time we are the victim of an offence or an act of aggression, a part of ourselves that lets itself be dragged down by the aggressor's action joins forces with the aggressor to become our persecutor. The damage this causes makes us dwell on the hurtful words and the images of the incident and rekindles the

One of the first conditions for forgiving ourselves is to start by forgiving ourselves for identifying with our offender.

emotions felt at the time of the offence. The damage seeps into our whole being, leaving us at risk of turning against ourselves and others the abuse of which we were originally victims.

In therapy, people often use the very words of their attacker to accuse themselves. One client repeated endlessly: "I am so stupid!" I would ask her to repeat this insult and to listen carefully to the tone of the voice that had called her "stupid." To her great surprise, she recognized that it belonged to her husband, who had hurled the insult at her as he walked out.

Consequently, one of the first conditions for forgiving ourselves is to start by forgiving ourselves for identifying with our offender.

THE RELATIONSHIP BETWEEN OURSELVES AND FORGIVENESS

The price we must pay for our lack of self-acceptance and self-esteem is very high. In *Man in Search of His Soul*, the great psychologist Carl Jung maintains that neurosis originates with a lack of self-acceptance and self-esteem: "Neurosis is inner cleavage — the state of being at war with oneself. Everything that accentuates this cleavage makes the patient worse, and everything that mitigates it tends to heal the patient," he wrote (236). This same author goes on to talk about loving ourselves: "The acceptance of oneself is the essence of the moral problem and the epitome of a whole outlook upon life. That I feed the hungry, that I forgive an insult, that I love my enemy in the name of Christ — all these are undoubtedly great virtues. What I do unto the least of my brethren, that I do unto Christ. But what if I should discover that the least amongst them all, the poorest of all the beggars, the most impudent of all the offenders, the very enemy of himself —

To forgive yourself is the condition of all other forgiveness.

that these are within me, and that I myself stand in need of the alms of my own kindness – that I myself am the enemy who must be loved?" (Ibid., p. 235).

We have to admit that we all must forgive ourselves on more than one account – for thinking we were all-powerful, for leaving ourselves open to injury by others, for letting the negative messages of our parents and teachers put us down, for letting our shadow turn against us and, finally, for conspiring with our offenders to the point where we perpetuate their offences within ourselves.

Faced with this enormous challenge of forgiving ourselves, we risk becoming discouraged, and maybe even despairing. With only our own initiative and strength to rely on, we would undoubtedly give way to them. The great French author of the nineteenth century Georges Bernanos suggested a similar conclusion: "Anyone who is forced to look at themselves without the 'gentle mercy of God' cannot help but fall into self-hatred and self-loathing" (Perrin 1987: 243).

Whatever else you retain from this chapter, I hope you will understand how vitally important it is to forgive yourself, for it is the condition of all other forgiveness. The Sufi sage Hasdai Ben Ha-Melekh asked: "How can we expect anyone who is cruel to himself to have compassion for others?"

Exercise

HELPING YOU FORGIVE YOURSELF

1. This first exercise will help you learn to treat yourself more gently. It is designed to help you become aware of all the times you blamed yourself and ordered yourself around, using expressions such as: "I have to … ," "I must … ," "I should … ," "I need to … ."

Start by drawing up a list of these expressions in your daily vocabulary. For instance: "I should forgive my spouse." Then, as you are making this list, take the time to stop at each expression and feel what is going on inside you. This will help you understand all these self-imposed demands as major sources of stress.

Once you have completed your list, replace each "I have to," "I should," "I must" by "I choose to" or "I am free to." Stop for a moment to enjoy the new state of mind this substitution produces.

2. This second exercise is designed to restore the inner harmony that the shock of the offence shattered. (Because the exercise is long, it would be preferable to tape it.)

Plan to eliminate all sources of distraction for twenty minutes. Sitting comfortably, back straight, take a few moments to enter into yourself.

First, become aware of the two parties in yourself: the accuser and the accused.

Place your hands on your knees and decide which hand will play the part of the accuser. Make sure that the other hand is ready to play the part of the accused. Many people find that the dominant hand plays the part of the accuser and the other that of the accused.

Once you have identified the two parties, raise the accusing hand to the side, above your head, bending your elbow to avoid getting too tired. Move it a little behind your head. Look at it carefully as if it were a screen from which your accusing self looks down. Describe him/her. (Pause) Which faces seem to be hiding behind this part of yourself that seems so demanding, tyrannical and creates so much guilt? (Pause) Listen to the voices accusing you. (Pause)

Now, place your fingers on your shoulder and, bending your elbow, let your arm relax.

Lift the other hand to the side, above your head and slightly behind it. This time look at the part of yourself that is the accused: the sensitive, tender, vulnerable part of yourself that tends to get depressed when blamed. How would you describe it? (Pause) How old is it? (Pause) How does it show up at various stages in your life? (Pause)

Place your fingers on your shoulder and let your arm relax.

Now, return your attention to the accuser. Lift your hand to the side and over your head. With your eyes once again focused on this accusing part of yourself, ask yourself the following: "Do I appreciate this part of myself, even though it seems to be so demanding and argumentative? (Pause) What positive motive could it have for behaving this way? (Pause) What would happen to me without it?" (Pause) Little by little, try to discover the positive intentions that drive it. Even if you do not always appreciate how it tries to help you, become aware that it means well.

Place your fingers on your shoulder and let your arm relax. Now go to the other hand. Lift it over your head, a little to the back. Ask yourself the same questions: "What do I most appreciate about this aspect of myself, despite its tremendous sensitivity and vulnerability? (Pause) What are its positive intentions towards me? (Pause) What would I do if I didn't

*have it?" (Pause) Little by little, become aware of its full impor-
tance to you, even if you don't always appreciate the methods it uses to get your love.*

*Let your hand rest on your shoulder. Come back to the other
hand, lifting it over your head, to the side and slightly to the
back. Ask its forgiveness for all the times you did not appreciate it and wanted to get rid of it.*

*Once you have received its forgiveness, tell it that you want
to forgive it for all the times it was too harsh and awkward
with you. Ask it to find other, more humane ways to better
achieve the results it expects.*

*Relax your hand and arm and, once again, talk to the tender
and sensitive part of yourself. Ask its forgiveness for all the
times you found it too sensitive and vulnerable, and you wanted to ignore it or get rid of it.*

*Once you have received its forgiveness, forgive it in turn for
all the suffering it caused you. Ask it to find more effective
ways to help you answer its needs.*

*Now extend both your hands in front of you, over your head,
keeping about a meter between them. Take a few moments
to reflect on the two parts of your being that they symbolize
and on all the riches, qualities and resources that each part
has to offer.*

*Once you feel ready, bring your hands towards each other at
your own pace. Continue to reflect on their identities. Once
they touch, interlace your fingers and bring your crossed
hands over your stomach. Then, enter deep within yourself.*

Without forcing it, trying to explain what's going on inside you or trying to figure out what is happening, keep these two parts together so that they can learn to recognize each other better, blend with each other, collaborate and work together in mutual respect.

Good. Now enter more deeply into yourself; surrender to the unconscious wisdom at work within you (at this point, you may invoke your spiritual source of inspiration). Ask it to harmonize the two parts of your self so that they live in peace, calm and serenity.

Savour this calm, this peace, this inner unity. While remaining relaxed and strong, imagine that you are looking into the eyes of the person who hurt you. For a few seconds, become aware of all you can teach that person. Then let their eyes disappear. Now enjoy the peace and deep unity you feel within yourself. These two parts of yourself will continue their reconciliation and integration in the days, weeks and months to come.

Choose some object in your home that symbolizes your current state of calm, joy and serenity. When you're at home, look at it; it will reawaken your current state of calm, peace and joy.

Then, at your own pace, return to the outside world. Count to ten to let yourself re-establish contact with the noises, lights and colours that surround you.

This exercise produces a deep sense of inner peace and harmony. You might wish to repeat it each day for several days. This new inner harmony will help you in the process of forgiving others.

3. The previous exercise was designed to restore your inner harmony. This exercise will let you experience forgiving yourself.

Take whatever time you need to go deep within yourself.

Renew your intention to feel free from all low self-esteem and self-hatred. Prepare to embrace yourself with love and compassion.

Ask God or your personal source of spiritual inspiration to accompany you in this process of forgiving yourself, and to fill your heart with strength and love.

The time has come to dispel all feelings of hostility, low self-esteem, and anger towards yourself. Let all these destructive feelings fade away.

Reject any temptation to put yourself down, argue with yourself, or compare yourself, favourably or unfavourably, with others.

Once and for all, give yourself permission to be yourself.

Recognize how painful it is to reject yourself and to live with a divided heart.

Slowly, invite your heart to take you back and love you again.

Very gently, listen to it tell the unloved part of yourself: "I forgive you for your weaknesses, your wounded humanity, your overblown ambitions, all your faults. I forgive you. I forgive you."

Let your heart say: "(your name: ... ...), welcome home. There's room for you here. I forgive you. I forgive you."

Good. Now, stop judging yourself negatively; stop being bitter towards yourself. Let go of any hard feelings towards yourself.

Continue to welcome your whole being tenderly and lovingly, as you would a child who has offended you. Make even more room in your heart and imagine it enveloping you in its light and warmth.

You may be bothered by feelings that you're being too self-indulgent. Accept these harsh thoughts that try to prevent you from forgiving yourself. Welcome them and let them melt in your heart's life-giving warmth.

Feel your heart become more tender towards you as it softens little by little.

Start to savour the joy of forgiving yourself and the birth of a new inner freedom. The relief you experience will help you understand that it is pointless to keep on being angry with yourself.

Let the understanding, self-esteem, peace and compassion in your heart fill your whole being.

Note how much more readily you are compassionate and forgiving towards others now that you have experienced the sense of liberation that comes from forgiving yourself.

Compassion for Yourself

I want to forgive myself

> *for reaching for the unreachable star*
>
> *for being fragile*
>
> *for being ashamed of my pain*
>
> *for blaming myself for my misery*
>
> *for striving after unattainable perfection*
>
> *for turning against myself along with my persecutor*
>
> *for closing my heart to myself*
>
> *for rehashing hurtful accusations others made against me*
>
> *for not being able to anticipate everything*
>
> *for hating myself.*

In short, I want to forgive myself for being human.

CHAPTER 14

Step Seven
Understand Your Offender

Forgiving allows you to suspend all judgment about the offender and to discover your real creative self, that is a spark of divinity.

— JOAN BORYSENKO

Understanding the offender means seeing them in a clearer light to catch all the facets of their person and the motives for their wrongdoing.

At a conference I was giving on the steps in the process of forgiveness, I noticed that one woman listened attentively; as soon as I broached this step, "Understanding your offender," she interrupted me: "I've been with you up to this point, but this is going too far; I don't want to try to understand my ex-spouse any more. I've already lost too much time at that little game." I responded readily: "You don't have to go through all of the steps to forgiveness all at once. Maybe you'd be better off going back to Step Five, accepting your anger." If, like my listener, you feel stuck at any given step, it would be useful to ask whether you might have skipped an earlier step. It is important to respect the pace at which you move along the path of forgiveness.

If your wound is still too raw, you would be undertaking this current step in vain, for it assumes that you have stopped being overly preoccupied with your pain. Do you feel ready to come out of yourself so you can change your perception of the person who hurt you?

Before we move on, I must remind you that understanding the offender does not mean excusing them, let alone clearing them from blame. Understanding the offender means seeing them in a clearer light to catch all the facets of their person and the motives for their wrongdoing.

Obviously, you will not understand everything about them and their behaviour. But the small amount of insight

I invite you to forgive with your eyes wide open so that you can see the big picture and discover aspects of your offender that you did not know.

that you draw from this step will make forgiving easier. Forgiveness will not seem like an unthinking or blind gesture, since you will have uncovered some of the "why's" behind the offensive behaviour. At the same time, you will be better disposed to change your picture of the offender and, consequently, forgiving will be easier. Contrary to those who advise you to close your eyes and forgive, I invite you to forgive with your eyes wide open so that you can see the big picture and discover aspects of your offender that you did not know.

NO MORE BLAMING

The humiliation and pain caused by the offence influence our perception of the offender and may even distort it. Then we are inclined to see the offender as loathesome, deceitful, aggressive, unfaithful, dangerous, threatening, hateful, irresponsible, and so on. Because the memory of the offending act not only dominates our memory, but fully preoccupies our thoughts, it conditions how we see the situation, to the point where we stop seeing the offender as a person who can change, and see them only in terms of the offence. The offender often becomes the personification of spite and meanness.

When this happens, we tend to get carried away by indignation and forget the words of the gospel: "Do not judge, so that you may not be judged" (Matthew 7.1). Note that the expression "Do not judge" does not mean "do not use your judgment" but rather do not use it to condemn another person. Furthermore, this command does not stem from an unfeeling, uncompromising moral obligation, but is first directed towards our own good: if I don't avoid condemning others, I won't avoid eventual condemnation myself. Why?

A large part of what I feel towards the other is often a part of myself that I refuse to recognize.

First, by condemning someone else, I risk losing sight of myself by focusing too much on the other's flaws. Then, blinded to my own flaws and weaknesses, I unconsciously project them onto others. If, on the other hand, I do not condemn others, I have a better chance of seeing both myself and, consequently, my offender more objectively. Was this not the message of Christ's metaphor: "Why do you see the speck in your neighbour's eye, but do not notice the log in your own eye?" (Matthew 7.3).

In a way, condemning my offender means condemning myself. A large part of what I feel towards the other is often a part of myself that I refuse to recognize. I then project onto my offender the sides of myself that are too painful to examine. The person I condemn reflects back to me those characteristics I dislike about myself. What if I were to attribute to myself those flaws and failings I see so readily in the offender? Only if I befriend what I fear in myself will I be able to grow. In reclaiming those aspects of myself that I consider weak and deficient, I become more complete and, hence, more myself. I will understand my offender only if I have first accepted in myself those weaknesses and flaws that I so clearly attribute to him or her.

When we reflect on it, we can see that the commandment to not condemn our offender melds with the commandment to "love your enemies." Here again, the teaching is not about moral obligation, but the desire for personal growth. For, in the context of forgiveness, the enemy or the offender reflects back to me my "shadow," those parts of myself that I do not like, that scare me or make me ashamed of myself. Hence, "loving your enemy" comes down to welcoming your shadow within yourself. Working at not condemning our enemies and

"Loving your enemy" comes down to welcoming your shadow within yourself.

loving them comes down to not condemning our shadow, but starting to befriend it and love it. In the act of forgiveness, non-judgment brings us to a reconciliation with our offender and, above all, with the dark side of ourselves that may prove to be a tremendous personal asset.

DISCOVERING MORE ABOUT THE OTHER'S BACKGROUND

"God forgives all, for he understands all," says an old adage. There is a profound truth here that we should definitely keep in mind as we attempt this step. Obviously a better understanding of a person's familial, social and cultural history helps in the process of forgiveness. Even if such conditioning does not justify inappropriate behaviour, at least it helps to explain it partially.

I discovered this while I was trying to understand my father's anxiety attacks and angry outbursts, which I found inexcusable. But my intolerant attitude changed once and for all following a conversation with my aunt about my father's childhood. From a very young age, my dad, who was the eldest in the family, had to assume the heavy responsibility of being the "man of the house" during his father's long absences. His constant fear and anxiety that he might not measure up to whatever situation he faced resulted from this background.

Once we know a person's background and history, we can put ourselves in their place and understand their unusual behaviours more easily. Knowing that a sexual abuser was the victim of abuse does not make the crime less serious, but it does allow us to treat the offender more compassionately.

*Once we know a
person's background
and history,
we can put ourselves
in their place and
understand their
unusual behaviours
more easily.*

LOOKING FOR THE OFFENDER'S POSITIVE MOTIVES

Virginia Satir, a family therapist for over forty years, had so much confidence in people that she was always looking for the positive motives behind her clients' actions, even the most sordid. She believed that all individuals exhibit an irrepressible desire for growth, even in their worst behaviours. She saw this positive motive as the rich inner resource that allowed her to connect with her clients and to begin forging behavioural change. Once the positive motive was uncovered, she would help her client become aware of it and appreciate its full worth. Then she would suggest constructive ways of fulfilling the desire for growth. For instance, she understood that the positive motive of someone who attempted suicide was to end suffering; of a violent father, to control his child; of a young shoplifter, to prove himself to his friends; of a rebellious child, to flaunt his power to his teachers.

This same positive motivation leads some people to believe that to help people mend their ways and make progress, they must inflict pain. How much humiliation is inflicted by teachers who are driven by the best intentions in the world! I remember well the day when the chapel master, after an hour of choir practice, pulled a piece of paper from his pocket and, in front of a choir of thirty singers, proceeded to read aloud: "Brothers André, Claude and Jean must withdraw immediately and indefinitely from the choir." Distressed, I immediately left the chapel. I still don't understand why this priest didn't let us know about our dismissal before the rehearsal. He certainly managed to humiliate me but he was mistaken if he thought he was teaching me humility. I also recall the high school English professor who would terrorize everyone with his

*We tend to reduce
offenders to their
destructive action
and, from that
point on, to have
a low opinion
of them.*

sarcasm as he read the worst compositions out to the whole class. We cannot shut our eyes to such blunders and their consequences for the victims. Still, as deplorable as their methods may be, these teachers may have been well-intentioned.

Although some may do harm through their good intentions, others do harm without wanting to: the drunk or drugged driver who kills or injures someone in an accident; the parents who unwittingly disrupt the lives of their children by their divorce; the caregivers who ruin the health of their patients by an incorrect diagnosis or treatment; the family breadwinner who jeopardizes the well-being of his wife and children with his business risks. In all of these cases, the victims suffer serious harm. While knowing that those responsible for the damage did not inflict it on purpose certainly cannot take away the pain and suffering, it can ease the reluctance to forgive.

DISCOVERING THE OFFENDER'S VALUE AND DIGNITY

We tend to reduce offenders to their destructive action and, from that point on, to have a low opinion of them. Yet, one wrong act is far from the last word on any human being: in spite of their faults, they are capable of change and reform. The deeper our disappointment in someone, the more we tend to see nothing but their faults, and the more we want to destroy them. The danger is even greater when we are dealing with someone we love who is close to us. The most stunning witness to this I have ever heard came from a woman whose personal and family life had been destroyed by her alcoholic husband. She told me that, even though she had decided to

Understanding the offender means accepting not being able to understand everything.

leave him, she never stopped loving him in spite of everything, and continued to admire him for his tenderness, his courage, his sense of humour and his deep religious faith. She added: "No one will be able to take from me the love and joy I shared with this man." Amazed, I watched her take leave of her marriage with dignity and a great deal of respect for her ex-husband. I saw her not as the victim still enslaved to her alcoholic husband, but as a free woman.

ACCEPTING THAT YOU WON'T UNDERSTAND EVERYTHING

Even if we wanted to know everything about our offenders, we would never be able to fully penetrate the secret of their being, or even discover all the motives behind their actions, motives of which they may often be unaware. Face-to-face with the mystery of a living person, we recognize that understanding the offender means accepting not being able to understand everything. At the end of a conference on forgiveness, one participant confided in me his philosophy of life: "If someone hurts me, I tell God: 'I don't understand why he did this to me, but I am confident that you do know.' And this reflection helps me maintain my inner peace." His wisdom echoes the thought of Dr. Philippe Madre: "Forgiving, in the end, is not an act of obliteration (in fact this is impossible since the wrong that I forgive will always be a part of my history), but an act of trust in the other, trust in the face of a certain amount of suffering, which is possible only with God's help" (1982: 187).

Exercise
UNDERSTANDING THE OFFENDER

The exercises I propose follow a certain logic. If you feel ill at ease and uncomfortable during an exercise, don't force yourself to keep going. By staying in touch with your discomfort or your inner resistance, you may be able to discover where you are in your journey to forgiveness. This awareness will help you to better situate and appreciate the next step to take in the right direction.

1. Focus and go into yourself. Use your imagination to picture your offender. Review everything you know about their personal history. If you feel strong enough, put yourself in their shoes: What would have happened to you if you had had to live through the same things?

2. Next, I invite you to discover the positive motives driving your offender's actions: self-protection, a need for power, a means of preserving dignity, etc. (Recognizing the positive motive does not mean that you agree with the offender's way of handling that motive.)

3. Make a list of the flaws you see in your offender, especially those that bother you the most. Then apply each of them to yourself. For instance, if you said: "I hate his aggressiveness," tell yourself: "I'm aggressive, too." Maybe you will discover in the flaw you condemn a part of yourself that you do not like. If so, first think about befriending it so you can integrate it into the rest of your personality. For instance: "I need to blend my excessive gentleness with more assertiveness."

CHAPTER 15

Step Eight
Make Sense of the Offence in Your Life

The challenge is to intertwine the flimsy threads of a shattered life in order to weave them into a masterpiece full of meaning and responsibility.

— GORDON ALLPORT

I invite you to discover the positive meaning of the offence or give it some meaning in your life.

Your journey to forgiveness has already covered many steps. Once you decided not to seek revenge, you decided to take a close look at yourself. Already you can feel your wound starting to heal. Your growing awareness and acceptance of your inner suffering have disposed you to understand your offender. In this way, you laid the groundwork and established the psychological conditions for forgiveness. In this eighth step, I invite you to go beyond the offence itself to discover the positive meaning of the offence or give it some meaning in your life. What will you make of this insult, this offence, this betrayal, this infidelity? How can it help you grow and find fulfillment?

What positive outcomes might result from the offence? How can you use this setback to your advantage? Its harmful effects are lasting only for those who refuse to move through the experience and instead sink into self-pity. Instead of giving in to this temptation, it is important to remember that hidden in every error or failure are elements of growth. To find the positive meaning of a failure, discover its hidden richness. Don't be swayed by those who say: "Nothing good can come of such misfortune." I can assure you that the opposite is true — your setback can become a source of growth. Many people have found that their lives take a new direction and their inner selves grow following tremendous hardship.

At this point, I realize that you may feel upset, annoyed or even angered by the invitation to find a positive meaning to your wound or its effects on your life. Such reactions indicate that you are not yet ready for this step. If you feel this way, I suggest you retrace some of the previous steps, and work with them some more until you have integrated them more deeply into your journey.

THE GOOD SIDE OF HAVING YOUR LIFE TURNED UPSIDE DOWN

Initially victims are shocked and deeply disturbed by the offence. They feel severely shaken up; their preconceived notions, set ideas, convictions, prejudices and life scripts have all been turned upside down. Yet, no matter how painful a situation may be, it always offers hope: a valuable moment of insight, a favourable occasion for breaking out of our typical short-sightedness. One of my professors maintained that very few people know how to make use of the richness and possibilities of reality. Most people bring stereotypical judgments to bear on events, which they see through the distorting lenses of their expectations, personal and cultural prejudices or pre-set opinions about their environment. Rather than trying to find the deeper meaning in an event, they settle for commonplace and generalized judgments such as "It's good," "It's bad," or "It's black," "It's white."

The following Chinese folk tale shows clearly how futile such judgments are. One day, a farmer loses the most superb of his stallions, a magnificent horse that ran away. His neighbours come to see him and commiserate on his misfortune: "How unlucky you are!" they tell him. He answers: "Maybe ... " The next day, his stallion reappears in its corral with three beautiful wild mares in tow. The neighbours rush over to congratulate him on his good fortune. Same laconic response: "Maybe … " One day, the farmer's son, attempting to tame one of the mares, breaks his leg. The neighbours immediately come to express their dismay over his misfortune. But, once again, the farmer reacts in the same way: "Maybe …" A few days later, a detachment of soldiers comes to mobilize the young men in the area. However, they are not interested in burdening themselves with the handicapped young man. "What good luck!" his neighbours exclaim. And all he says is: "Maybe … "

Our prejudices and preconceived ideas about people and events often lead us to feel disappointed and frustrated. We "know" how parents should behave with their children, spouses with their partners, bosses with their employees, God with the world, and so on. We forget that our own perspectives often blind us or limit our vision.

The shock of the offence saves us by stripping away our blinders and forcing us out of rigid notions. This is even truer when someone we love hurts us; the offended party, frustrated by unrealistic expectations, has to get rid of them so they can come to appreciate and love that relative or friend for who they really are.

THE GOOD THINGS THAT COME FROM A LOSS

In the conferences I give, I often urge my listeners to reflect upon what they have gained from the experience of being injured, insulted, or victimized by infidelity or injustice. I invite them to ask themselves: "What have you learned from this experience? How have you grown as a result of this ordeal? To what extent has your life taken a new direction?"

Here are a few of their replies:

"I know myself a lot better."

"I have gained more inner freedom."

"It has made me aware of my values. After my divorce, I noticed that I could be myself more easily and live according to my values."

"My heartbreak taught me to better know myself. Now, instead of depending on the love of others, I have started to love myself."

"It's over. Never again will I let anyone hurt me. I'm going to learn to protect myself better."

"I've learned to say 'no' when something doesn't fit with my values."

"When my wife left me, I told myself: 'I no longer have a choice; I have to clean up my act.' Then, in spite of my pride, I asked for help for the first time in my life."

"My ordeal wove me a loving heart."

"I have a lot more compassion and understanding for others."

"I have stopped running after alcoholic husbands to try to save them. I've become aware that I was the one needing help."

"In my despair, I discovered God's love and steadfastness — after I got really angry at him."

When I question people about how their lives have changed for the better after they've been hurt, I am always stunned by the variety and quality of their responses. Sometimes the positive effect of the offence and injustice of which they were victims appears spontaneously. At other times, they discover and deepen their understanding of the positive outcomes over a period of weeks, or even months. Initially, these people saw their lives as an indecipherable puzzle, but once they uncover some meaning in the offence, a new vision of life begins to take shape.

WHEN THE OFFENCE HELPS YOU GET TO KNOW YOURSELF

Only you can find meaning in your loss, but this doesn't mean someone can't encourage you to look for it. Unfortunately, few are the guides who know how to lead you to a greater awareness of yourself and awaken you to the possibilities of growth that unhappiness presents.

A serious injustice or offence may mark the point of departure of an enriching human adventure that unfolds in three stages. In the first stage, we have to grieve our life before the offence. The second stage, liminal or "in-between time," gives us the opportunity to understand ourselves and our future prospects better. This "in-between time" is fundamental and definitive. We have to give ourselves over to it fully before we can participate in the third stage: reorganizing our life in anticipation of a new beginning.

The big danger here is neglecting the decisive in-between stage: either we are tempted to settle into the past, or we try to move immediately to the new beginning of life. Both choices will inevitably fail.

Why is the in-between time so important? Once the wound is less raw and all-absorbing, it is important to comto terms with what happened: "How did I manage to put myself in such a vulnerable situation?" The detachment brought on by the offence helps us let go of our illusions and impossible expectations of ourselves and others. More than ever, we are brought face to face with ourselves and realize that the positions and roles we have previously assumed lose their importance. Confronted by the emptiness around us, we are forced to ask ourselves the fundamental question: "Who am I?" No one else can answer this question, not even our psychologist or spiritual director. This questioning of our true identity will doubtless include moments of solitude, anguish and fear of being wrong. But if we persevere, we will see how much this moment of reflection can give birth to new and fruitful self-understanding.

During this "in-between time," a third question comes to the foreground: "What do I want to do with my life?" "What new reasons for living can I find in this?" Here again, we can find the answers to these questions only within us. All we need is the courage and patience to welcome them as they emerge.

Suffering an injustice or an offence is not a pleasant experience. Once the trauma has passed, the experience makes us confront ourselves and our own inner freedom. We must choose between being victimized and reacting. If you decide to react, you open yourself to the possibility of discovering your real identity and forming new bonds with others. In other words, you have found meaning in your suffering. This is the message of Dr. Victor Frankl's famous book, *Man's Search for Meaning*. He knew of what he spoke, for he had endured profound suffering and humiliation in the concentration camps of World War II without letting himself be beaten. He wrote: "The important thing is to call on the highest potential of man, that of transforming personal tragedy into victory, suffering into human achievement" (1988: 121).

Exercise
DISCOVERING THE POSITIVE
MEANING OF THE INJURY

At this point, I am proposing a series of questions that will help you work out the positive meaning of your injury. It is important to let yourself hear these questions; some will doubtless speak louder than others. Be attentive to the answers your inner voice offers without trying to censor them. Sometimes an answer evolves; only with time will you discover its full meaning and significance. Throughout the exercise, it would be helpful to record your observations in your journal.

What have I learned from the injury I suffered?

What have I learned about myself?

What limits or weaknesses have I discovered in myself?

Have I become more human?

What new resources and strengths have I found in myself?

What new level of maturity have I reached?

What new possibilities has this ordeal opened up for me?

What new reasons for living have I discovered?

To what point has my injury allowed the depths of my soul to emerge?

To what extent have I decided to change my relationship with others, especially with God or my higher power?

How will I now continue my life journey?

With what important contemporary, historical or mythological figure has this experience made me identify?

CHAPTER 16

Step Nine
Recognize That You're Worthy of Forgiveness –
and Already Forgiven

Only those who have experienced forgiveness can truly forgive.

— GEORGE SOARES-PRABHU

You are worthy of forgiveness; you have been forgiven many times in the past.

As you make your inner journey on the path to forgiveness, you are slowly realizing that the act of forgiveness depends as much on human effort as on spiritual gifts. You are discovering that forgiveness is both a human task accomplished through your psychological effort and a divine gift that compensates for your weaknesses. Undoubtedly in your work on forgiveness to this point, you have touched your personal limits and felt the need for special help. Now, your journey will take you deeper into the spiritual universe, where you are not so much called upon to act as to let yourself be acted upon. Your own efforts become less important than being humbly open to patiently welcome God's presence. When your journey of forgiveness enters the spiritual realm, you relinquish initiative and control to relax and let yourself be filled with God's presence.

This chapter is designed to let you recognize not only that you are worthy of forgiveness, but also that you have been forgiven many times in the past. This awareness will help you forgive, for, in this, forgiveness is a lot like love. People who are incapable of letting themselves be loved or of realizing that they are loved, are unable to love others. Similarly, if people who want to forgive cannot feel that they have been forgiven, how will they be able to forgive? My challenge to you, then, is to let go of all your resistance to letting yourself be loved deeply and forgiven by others, especially God.

WE NEED TO EXPERIENCE FORGIVENESS
SO WE CAN FORGIVE

The story of Corrie Ten Boom illustrates the need to have experienced another's forgiveness before we can forgive someone else. Corrie was released from a Nazi concentration camp shortly after the Allied invasion of Germany. It took her a long time to free herself of her unspoken hatred toward her persecutors. One day, she decided to let forgiveness heal her. Once she was sure that she had totally freed herself of her hatred and had forgiven, she came up with the idea of a huge project to heal the wounds and enmities that World War II had caused in these countries. Thus she launched a crusade through several countries, preaching the creative force of forgiveness and love.

She was not afraid of taking her message to Germany. One night, in Munich, after speaking to a group of Germans who were searching for forgiveness, she had a gut-wrenching experience that put the power of her own forgiveness to the test. A man came up to her, held out his hand and said: "Ja, Fraülein Ten Boom, I am so happy to hear you say that Jesus forgives all our sins."

Corrie immediately recognized him as one of the guards from the concentration camp. She remembered how he had humiliated her and her fellow prisoners by forcing them to shower naked under his disdainful "superman" gaze. Just as she was about to shake his hand, Corrie suddenly felt hers freeze at her side. Instantly aware of her inability to forgive him, she was at once stunned and terrified. She had thought that she was fully healed of her wound, that she had overcome her hatred and had forgiven. But at that moment, face to face with one of her persecutors, she was overwhelmed by contempt and hatred. Paralyzed, she did not know what to say or do.

So, she started to pray: "Jesus, I feel powerless to forgive this man. Forgive me." At that very instant, something marvellous happened to her. She felt touched by Jesus' forgiveness. Her hand rose and she took that of her former torturer. At that very moment, she freed herself and her persecutor from her horrible past.

How do we explain such a sudden turnaround? You guessed it. The miracle of forgiveness happened to Corrie thanks to the indescribable feeling that Jesus had forgiven her for her inability to forgive. Her own admission of powerlessness had softened her heart so that she could receive the grace of forgiveness.

DESCRIBING THE FEELING OF BEING WORTHY OF FORGIVENESS

Words cannot begin to express the nature, depth and intensity of the experience of forgiveness. It cannot be compared to any other experience, whether it be passionate love, gratitude, joy, success, or reunion with friends. Somehow it touches the ego in its very depth. For this reason, it can be called a foundational experience.

Lewis Smedes (1984: 118) calls it "fundamental feeling." Fundamental because, more than any other experience, it gives the sense of being recognized and appreciated for who we are in the very depths of our being. Then we feel unconditionally loved in spite of our ugliness, weaknesses, failures, or transgressions. We can say at that moment that the ego knows that it is bound to and inseparable from the Source of love. This feeling can be compared to the security and trust experienced

We can come back anytime to refresh ourselves at this source and be strengthened in love.

by children who are loved and wanted by their parents just for who they are. Even though we may feel enormous guilt about our faults or mistakes, the feeling that we have been forgiven is even stronger. It assures us that we will never again lose this source of infinite love. We know that we can come back anytime to refresh ourselves at this source and be strengthened in love.

Yet, we sometimes lose this "fundamental feeling." I know from personal experience that finding it again is a very moving experience. During a study session on the use of story in pastoral work, to a room filled with over 400 priests, ministers, religious men and women and pastors, John Shea, a theologian famous for his storytelling abilities, told the parable of the prodigal son. I was not really interested when he started. But as I let myself be carried along by the storyteller, tears welled up in my eyes. And I was not alone! When I emerged from his spell, I glanced around and noticed that nearly everyone in the hall was crying; some were sobbing so hard that their neighbours had to comfort them. Thanks to his dramatic talent, Shea had managed to make his audience relive two opposing feelings: the tremendous desire to know that we are loved and forgiven, and the conviction that we are not worthy of it.

But we cannot summon such feelings at will. And not everyone can feel loved to the point of forgiveness. The only thing we can do is to prepare ourselves to receive this special grace that is closely related to conversion. The gospel teaches us that those who let themselves be loved in spite of their poverty are saved, while the hearts of those who have refused love and forgiveness are hardened. On the one hand, we see those who let the merciful love of Christ touch them: Mary

Why do we resist being touched by the grace of forgiveness?

Magdalen, Zacchaeus, Matthew, and the Samaritan; on the other hand, we have the scribes and the Pharisees, Simon and the merciless tax collector who, along with so many other "upstanding" individuals, remain closed to love and forgiveness.

OBSTACLES TO RECOGNIZING HOW MUCH WE'RE LOVED

Why do we resist being touched by the grace of forgiveness? To understand, we'll examine four kinds of people whom forgiveness can't reach. We may recognize ourselves among them.

There are those who see themselves as unforgivable. They think that their transgressions are so overwhelming that they can never be forgiven. There seem to be fewer and fewer such people in our secular society.

Then there are those who do not believe that love is unmerited, freely given. In principle they accept that love can be unconditional, but they do not believe it in practice. They are convinced that nothing is free and that sooner or later you have to pay for everything, including forgiveness. Often, these people grew up with parents who never showed them unconditional love. They were loved only as a reward for high marks in school, good behaviour or services rendered.

A third category of people rejects forgiveness. They simply don't feel the need for it because they seem to experience no individual or social guilt. They live in a sort of moral and spiritual vacuum; their lack of spiritual and moral anchors makes them insensitive to any need for forgiveness. Would this not apply to many of those around us? Some thinkers go so far as to maintain that this lack of moral awareness lies behind many of the suicides by young people (Peters 1986: 20).

Those who do not love themselves and do not forgive themselves will not be able to love or to forgive others either.

In the last category, I would include all those who simply reject guilt as a psychological flaw. Some schools of psychology consider that guilt feelings and the need for forgiveness indicate a lack of maturity and autonomy. This confuses obsessive and pathological feelings of guilt with healthy feelings of guilt. While neurotic guilt tyrannizes and crushes, healthy and normal feelings of guilt alert us to our real situation: we are limited and fallible beings. Such a truthful self-awareness is liberating, for it can help us establish a more realistic moral ideal.

To let ourselves be forgiven without feeling humiliated or diminished: that is a challenge. Many turn down forgiveness to avoid being humiliated. Philippe Le Touzé describes the workings of God's forgiveness in the characters of Georges Bernanos, and highlights this refusal: "Human beings shut themselves off from forgiveness which humiliates them and robs them of the illusion of autonomy, thus putting them at the mercy of another; hence the modern movement to recreate a universe with no God" (Perrin 1987: 237). A distorted view of autonomy pushes us into acts of false independence, while true autonomy enables us to choose our dependencies.

In brief, it seems obvious that those who do not love themselves and do not forgive themselves will not be able to love or to forgive others either. Furthermore, loving ourselves and forgiving ourselves seem unrealistic and illusory without the kindness of the Other. The ability to accept that our sins have been forgiven by the God who looks on us in love seems to be the only form of self-love that lets us forgive those who have sinned against us.

Exercise

COMING TO ACCEPT FORGIVENESS

1. Letting yourself be loved in the experience of forgiveness is not easy. To help you with this, I propose an exercise designed to help you simply *receive*. Some active and generous people have never learned to receive, much less to let themselves be spoiled. They feel more in control and sure of themselves when they are giving. They do not tolerate well the feelings of dependence that come from receiving.

Take time to delight in all the pleasant sensations that life has to offer you today: the smell of toast, the aroma of coffee, the heat of the sun, the sight of a beautiful landscape, the shapes of trees, the colours of the season, the feeling of being alive, the sound of a beautiful piece of music, etc. Let yourself revel in these sensations, if only for a few minutes a day.

2. This second exercise is designed to develop your capacity for *receiving*.

Settle into a comfortable position. Then, recall the signs of caring you received throughout the day: greetings, compliments, faces that lit up when they saw you, thank yous, joyful greetings from your pet, a letter from a friend, etc. How did you receive these everyday gifts? Did you take time to let the joy of receiving sink in, so that it could take root in your emotional life and you could celebrate it?

3. This exercise is taken from my book *To Love Again*. I call it "Litanies of Love."

Settle into a relaxed position and make sure there are no distractions. Start by reciting to yourself the list of people,

157

*animals, plants and objects that love you. For instance:
John loves me, my mother loves me, God loves me, my
friend Arthur loves me, my pet loves me, the sun loves me,
the breeze loves me, my painting loves me, etc. Make your
way through, without worrying about the degree or quan-
tity of love. The important thing is to become aware of the
many forms of love that surround you.*

4. Make a list of people who have forgiven your mistakes,
weaknesses and faults in the past. This will help you know
that you deserve forgiveness and have been forgiven. Once you
have completed the list, take the time to come back to each
instance of forgiveness received. Savour each one. Then, let
your sense of worth wash over you and ignore any feelings
that might diminish it.

5. Take the time to meditate on these words of St. John: "and
by this we will know that we are from the truth and will reassure our hearts before him whenever our hearts condemn us;
for God is greater than our hearts, and he knows everything"
(I John 3.19-20).

CHAPTER 17

Step Ten
Stop Trying So Hard to Forgive

But do not do his will relentlessly and tensely.
Relax. Let go. Give yourself over to God.

— THOMAS KELLY

You must give up the desire to be the sole architect of the forgiveness you offer.

Up to this point, you have invested much effort in walking the "uncertain path" of forgiveness. The title of this chapter may surprise you, then: stop trying so hard to forgive. As you are moving more deeply into the spiritual stage of forgiveness, you are realizing that sheer willpower could harm you rather than help you. The time has now come for you to let go of all subtle pride and every instinct for control that you may be tempted to cling to in the act of forgiveness. Stubbornly wanting to rely only on your own resources in the process of forgiveness suggests an unhealthy focus on yourself. Therefore you must give up the desire to be the sole architect of the forgiveness you offer and, following from that, any personal power you stand to gain from it.

This detachment will help you get rid of any false motives for forgiving that you may have constructed, so they do not spoil the beauty and authenticity of your action. As you do this, you are creating the free space within yourself that the grace of forgiveness needs to do its work.

During this step, you will learn to let go of all desire for self-importance, for it is incompatible with forgiveness. You will even get ready to give up the desire for personal perfection, no matter how praiseworthy it may be, so that divine inspiration can move through you freely. You are still

In forgiveness, we give up acting on our own so we can be part of God's action.

sailing your ship in the bay of forgiveness, but you've stopped rowing to let divine breezes guide you instead.

From the moment you decided to forgive, you had to demand a great deal of personal asceticism of yourself. But forgiveness is not born of our own efforts at asceticism; rather it is born of our relationship with God, because it is of a different nature. In forgiveness, we give up acting on our own so we can be part of God's action. On the cross, Jesus, rather than forgive his persecutors himself, asked God to do it: "Father, forgive them, for they know not what they do" (Luke 23.34).

STUBBORNNESS: AN OBSTACLE TO FORGIVENESS

The idea that we must give up our stubborn determination to forgive came to me after I heard the story of a religious missionary who had doggedly driven himself to forgive through sheer willpower. This missionary had dedicated himself, heart and soul, to the evangelization of his adopted people. But not everyone appreciated his methods, which some people misrepresented. These tales found their way to the ears of his provincial superior, who got nervous and ordered the missionary to return home as quickly as possible. It is easy to see why, after so many years of dedication, the man was completely taken aback at having his whole missionary career crumble before his eyes.

After a few months of rest and reflection, he found that he wanted to be free of the exhausting resentment that was poisoning his life. He decided to forgive his former Provincial for the wrong and suffering he had inflicted on him. He started by praying and having prayers said for him. Several times a day, he would say "I forgive you," as he thought of his former

*He opened himself
to receive the grace
of forgiveness
without knowing
how, when or
where it would
be granted him.*

Provincial. But his effort was wasted; nothing eased his bitterness. His determination to forgive only deepened his resentment.

Now somewhat desperate, the missionary resorted to the ultimate solution: a silent retreat for the sole purpose of achieving forgiveness. He set about his self-appointed task immediately: he read about forgiveness, spent long hours in the chapel and repeated the formula "I forgive you." Sometimes he thought he had attained his goal only to wake up the very next day with the same sting in his heart. On the night of the fourth day, as he was meditating in the chapel, he instinctively picked up the New Testament, opened it at random, and came across the passage about the healing of the crippled man. The Pharisees' comment "God alone can forgive," jumped out at him. At that moment he understood the uselessness of trying to forgive while relying only on himself. He finally understood that he was being driven by the desire for power. His great efforts had only served to cover up his humiliation and anger. Suddenly he recognized that he had not acknowledged that he really wanted to appear morally superior to his former Provincial and subtly take revenge on him.

This discovery enabled him to give himself up to God completely. He started by relaxing. Then he opened himself to receive the grace of forgiveness without knowing how, when or where it would be granted him. Two days later, he had the feeling, a bit confused at first, then more and more distinct, that something had unravelled inside him. From that moment on, he felt peace washing over him; his heart felt lighter, his soul, liberated. Curiously, he no longer felt the need to repeat his incantation: "I forgive you." Resentment had released its stranglehold and forgiveness had finally found a home in him.

Only when it comes from a heart that is free and forgiven can forgiveness spring forth.

DON'T REDUCE FORGIVENESS TO A MORAL OBLIGATION

Here is another reason to give up trying to forgive through sheer willpower. Forgiveness cannot be the object of a commandment or moral law. It is easy to fall into this trap and to keep forgiveness from being spontaneous and free to those who ask. This is what St. Peter had so much trouble understanding when he asked Jesus: "Lord, when my brother wrongs me, how many times shall I forgive him? Up to seven times?" Preoccupied as he was with legalistic concepts, Peter was hoping to find precise rules on forgiveness to guide his moral judgment. Reversing the advice of Lamek, who called for seventy-fold vengeance, Jesus replied: "I do not say seven times, but seventy times seven" (Matthew 18.21-22). Jesus' answer makes it very clear that forgiveness finds its source, not in a moral obligation, but rather in the mystery of the intimate relationship between God and human beings. Far from being a command, forgiveness arises from a conversion of the heart and the choice of a lifestyle that reflects how God acts. Yet who could claim God's life as the source of their living without having first received it as a gift? Only when it comes from a heart that is free and forgiven can forgiveness spring forth.

To listen to some preachers and "spiritual masters," we would be inclined to think the opposite. They insist so forcefully on the obligation to forgive that they give the impression that forgiveness is nothing more than the fruit of a generous will in which divine grace plays no part. Such statements trap their listeners and readers in delusions of grandeur about their capacity to forgive. It is hardly surprising that repeated failures to forgive eventually leave many of them discouraged.

People lost sight of the fact that God's love towards sinners is a complete gift.

In matters of forgiveness, some of the church's practices have also gotten off course. We have only to think about the directives handed out once upon a time for the administration of the sacrament of forgiveness. They reflect a far too juridical and legalistic mentality. People talked about tribunals of penitence, the confessor as judge, the obligation to go to confession, the need for painstaking confession of all of one's sins. It is hardly surprising that, in the end, people lost sight of the fact that God's love towards sinners is a complete gift. It is possible that a certain legalistic theology of forgiveness has contributed in part to the general disillusionment with the sacrament of reconciliation, whose importance for spiritual growth cannot be underestimated. Carl Jung was absolutely correct when he wrote that those who cannot unveil their conscience to another are destined to "spiritual isolation."

Exercise

PRAYER FOR THE AFFIRMATION OF FORGIVENESS

Earlier I mentioned that to forgive effectively, we need to give up our desire for power. This is possible only through prayer said in utter confidence that it will be answered. Without this confidence, forgiveness cannot be effective. Mark's gospel stressed its importance: "If you do not doubt in your heart, but believe that what you say will come to pass, it will be done for you" (Mark 11.23). Therefore I am suggesting a prayer experience that leaves little room for doubt and hesitation because it affirms in advance that the prayer is already heard. In other words, I suggest you look at forgiveness as an intrinsic event that has already happened. Don't feel that you must use the prayer formulas suggested here; you are certainly free to create your own prayer of affirmation.

Affirmation Prayer

Dim the lights or light a candle.

Seat yourself comfortably in a quiet spot.

Place yourself in the presence of God (or your own spiritual source).

Ask God to let you live the experience of forgiveness now.

You have forgiven your offender. Become aware of this; hear yourself and see yourself in this situation:

> *I feel free of all resentment.*
>
> *No anguish is restricting my throat.*
>
> *My heart grows lighter and happier.*
>
> *My breathing is deeper and my hands are warmer.*

My feet are resting on solid ground.

I already feel free of the weight of the offence.

An interior dialogue is starting up in me.

I hear God speaking: "You are precious in my sight, and honoured, and I love you."

I savour these words. I hear God say to me: "You are free of all anguish and suffering. You are entering a new phase in your life. From your past errors, you learn wisdom as you get to know yourself better. Your wound is transformed now into a source of new life and maturity."

The inner dialogue continues: "Every day, I become more and more important in my eyes. I will never betray myself again. From now on, I shall be my best friend. I will love others as I love myself. The one who hurt me will receive that same love, too."

I notice that my wound has become a nicely healed scar.

My memories of the hurt no longer disturb me; I can actually recall the circumstances of the offence without feeling their sting.

I am prepared to discover beauty in all people, including my offender.

I am standing, tall, proud, free and freed, before my offender who has now become my neighbour.

I am becoming more and more understanding towards myself and others.

I see and feel God's forgiveness penetrating me more deeply and radiating to others. The reflection of God's love for me and for the one who hurt me shines brightly for all to see.

At the end of this prayer, resume your normal routine, confident that the world is different since you experienced the effects of forgiveness in you and in the other.

CHAPTER 18

Step Eleven
Open up to the Grace of Forgiving

*It is in the heart of forgiveness that Creation is
reborn in its initial purity.*

— PHILIPPE LE TOUZÉ

*In theory it is
easy to believe that
God is loving and
merciful. In fact
it is not so easy.*

The inner emptiness you created by surrendering the desire to be the one and only author of your forgiveness allows you to receive divine love. Moved by God, you prepare yourself to forgive. You respond to Jesus' invitation: "Be merciful, just as our Father is merciful" (Luke 6.36). Rather than playing God by relying on nothing but your own strengths, you open yourself to receive God's life, which is the source of love and forgiveness.

Even after you ask for God's help, you may still feel hesitant or powerless to forgive. Why? False images of God that conceal from you the real face of the God of love and compassion may lie at the root of this difficulty.

FROM GOD AS DISPENSER OF JUSTICE, TO THE REAL GOD

In theory it is easy to believe that God is loving and merciful. In fact it is not so easy (Duquoc 1986: 35). Being able to actually live out of this experience of the divine demands hard spiritual and emotional work. Our religious imagination is often hard pressed to distinguish the God of love and mercy from the God who administers justice.

In my clinical practice, I have often had to help my clients distinguish between the God of justice and the God of love. The following story may clarify this. Following the death of her mother, a nun was haunted by the notion that the full

I believed it was a priority that she free herself once and for all from this image of God.

force of God's punishment had just fallen on her. She was both distressed and humiliated at being the victim of such an obsession. As a religion teacher, she taught her students about a loving and merciful God, yet her gut feeling was that she was being pursued by an interfering, vengeful God, all because she had not been a "good sister." She was quite aware of the incompatibility between the two points of view.

Initially, our work in therapy dealt primarily with her grief for her mother. Once we had worked this through properly, I found the right moment to bring up her notion of a vengeful God and the guilt crisis it had sparked. Although my client was rather annoyed at this reminder, I decided to ask her if the episodes of guilt she was experiencing were isolated reactions or ongoing tendencies. After letting me know that I was attaching far too much importance to such an insignificant event, she admitted that during times of crisis, she was obsessed by the thought of a God who punishes. When she brought this up with her spiritual directors, they advised her to meditate on God's goodness and to stop feeling guilty, advice that had proved ineffective.

I explained to my client that I believed it was a priority that she free herself once and for all from this image of God that was incompatible with her life of prayer and her work as a religion teacher. She thus asked me to help her eliminate this God of punishment from her life. I knew that not only can a person not get rid of such a serious psychological complex, but that they should not even attempt it. My client had to learn to bring it under control and live with it. This is why I asked her to start by initiating a dialogue with it.

This is exactly what she did on retreat. To her great surprise, behind this strange image of God, she recognized that

We cannot work out of our childish images of God forever.

of her mother. From the time my client was very young, her mother had drilled into her a sickly fear of God. She often talked about family and friends whom God was punishing for disobedience. As liberating as it was, this discovery saddened her deeply because she realized at the same time that a big part of her life was dominated by the image of this strict and menacing God.

In the following days, she continued her dialogue with her God of judgment and punishment. She asked him to make way, little by little, for the God of love of Jesus Christ and to stop coming between her and this God, especially at times of crisis. Furthermore, she reassured her punitive, judgmental God that she appreciated his positive attempts to make her into a person with faultless morals.

This story shows how important it is to carefully examine our notion of God and to correct it, if necessary, if we want to be worthy of forgiveness and able to forgive. We cannot work out of our childish images of God forever. How can we forgive if we take a false God as a model: a pitiless judge, a perfectionist teacher, a detached character, a fearful moralizer? These gods make it impossible for their followers to grant forgiveness.

GOD'S LOVE IS NOT CONSTRAINED BY HUMAN FORGIVENESS

But these are not the only false images of God that get in the way of forgiveness. There is also that of the god whose own acts of forgiveness are conditioned by human acts of forgiveness: God will forgive me only if I have forgiven someone else. I have encountered this way of thinking about forgiveness, which is very widespread, among most of the participants in

From the concept of God's unmerited forgiveness, we have slid, little by little, to a notion of forgiveness as reward for our acts of forgiveness.

my workshops on forgiveness. They believe the words of the Our Father back up their position: "Forgive us our trespasses as we forgive those who trespass against us."

How do we explain why faithful Christians have arrived at such a notion of divine forgiveness? Did a certain strand of Christian tradition lose the original gospel message? From the concept of God's unmerited forgiveness, we have slid, little by little, to a notion of forgiveness as reward for our acts of forgiveness. This picture set limits on God's love which would no longer take the initiative to forgive. Rather, it tags along behind our miserly human acts of forgiveness.

The concept of God's forgiveness as a form of retributive justice is that much more likely because we find traces of it in Matthew's gospel: "For if you forgive others their trespasses, your heavenly Father will also forgive you; but if you do not forgive others, neither will your Father forgive your trespasses" (Matthew 6.14-15). Some biblical scholars interpret this statement in light of the fact that Matthew is addressing listeners who are still steeped in the Old Testament law. Even if elsewhere he clearly affirms that salvation is unearned, a legalistic spirit dominates Matthew's whole line of rabbinical thinking. This is the line of thought that is found in his understanding of forgiveness. We might add that the influence of his gospel has weighed in more heavily in the development of a Christian mentality since, up until the 1960s and the second Vatican Council, it was the texts of Matthew that were read almost exclusively at Sunday liturgies. So, it is hardly surprising that followers came to think that they could obtain God's forgiveness by the merits of their own acts of forgiveness. Thus, forgiveness became a sort of subtle barter between God and humans.

Forgiveness is not an act of will that depends only on human effort.

The idea of a bargaining god does not fit well with God's infinite mercy. This negative view of God has created a great deal of confusion and a major impasse in spiritual life, especially among those who feel unable to forgive. To secure the salvation which comes from God's forgiveness, they think they have to make themselves forgive at any cost, even if they often feel unable to do so. Either they admit that they cannot forgive, and that thus they are unworthy to receive God's forgiveness because of their lack of generosity, or they lie to themselves so they can offer false, or at least insincere, forgiveness. We see what an agonizing dilemma this creates for those who believe they can earn God's forgiveness.

How do people get out of this impasse? The only way is to hold fast to two truths. The first one is that God always takes the initiative in forgiveness, just as God is the only one who takes the initiative in love. St. John does not hesitate to affirm this: "In this is love, not that we loved God, but that he loved us" (I John 4.10). The second truth flows from the first. Forgiveness is not an act of will that depends only on human effort and that ought to be applied in the name of who knows what precept or law. Above all, it is the fruit of a conversion of heart, an opening up to the grace of forgiveness. This conversion, although it may be immediate and spontaneous in some cases, normally emerges, ripens and develops over a relatively long period of time.

If we were not convinced of these two truths, we would only have to read the parable of the bankrupt creditor (Matthew 18.23-25). This is the story of a master who takes the initiative to forgive one of his debtors a rather heavy debt. But it so happens that the latter does not offer the same mercy to a poor man who owes him a small amount of

While God takes the initiative in granting forgiveness, God cannot force anyone to accept it.

money. We know the rest of the story. The master, on learning of the harshness and strictness of the bankrupt debtor, has him thrown into prison until he can repay his entire debt.

Remember two points in this parable about forgiveness. First, it is the master [God] who takes the initiative to perform a merciful act. Second, the debtor who has been so blessed refuses to be moved or influenced by his creditor's generosity. Being moved in this way would certainly have brought him to forgive his own debtor, but he failed to show the same magnanimity. He did not absorb his master's forgiveness at any deep level that would have allowed him to be transformed and capable of performing a similar act of mercy. Thus he condemns himself.

Here we stand before the mystery of human freedom that can bring us to even refuse grace. While God takes the initiative in granting forgiveness, God cannot force anyone to accept it. In a way, God is powerless when people reject his "forgiveness of debts," his forgiveness. In contrast to the master in the parable, God would undoubtedly be more patient and would know to wait for the favourable moment for opening up even the hardest heart.

THE HUMBLE FORGIVENESS OF THE GOD OF JESUS

But who is the real God of forgiveness? To fully understand the divine ways of forgiveness, we need only look at how Jesus acted towards "sinners." He is not haughty, moralizing or disdainful towards them. Rather, he is simple, humble and understanding. He takes the initiative to visit people who are imprisoned by their sins. Once he is with them, he validates them by setting up a situation in which he receives from them.

*How do we do
as God does?*

He asks the Samaritan woman for water; when he sees Zacchaeus, he invites himself into his home; he allows Mary Magdalen to bathe his feet in perfume. Even before he speaks of forgiveness, he starts by establishing a person-to-person relationship. Through this basic contact Jesus manifests his forgiveness.

How do we open up to God's forgiveness? How do we do as God does? Jacques-Marie Pohier offers this good news: "The God of the Bible shows us both that he is vulnerable — the father of the prodigal child, or the one who sets off to find the lost sheep — and that he refuses our payment. This is an unbearable paradox for us. Furthermore, I do not think that we can come close to imitating God's forgiveness. All we can do is hope that by being around God a lot, some of God may eventually rub off on us … " (Pohier 1977: 218).

Exercise

OPENING UP TO THE GRACE OF FORGIVENESS

As with the other exercises, make yourself comfortable and get away from any distractions. You may find it helpful to tape this exercise.

Let yourself be guided by the imagery. As you listen to its words, remember to respect your own rhythm.

Take some time to go inside yourself and connect with your symbolic and sacred world. Close your eyes if this helps.

You are in a field of flowers bathed in sunshine. Take the time to contemplate the scenery and taste the freshness of the surroundings.

In the distance, you see a house surrounded by an unusual light. You head towards it. You discover a stone staircase leading down into a basement. One by one, you walk down the seven steps. There in front of you stands a thick oak door with finely sculpted, graceful motifs. Your curiosity overtakes you; you push the door open and walk through it. You find yourself in a room lit up by a strange glow. To your great surprise, you see a double of yourself tied to a chair. Take the time to closely examine the bindings. Which parts of your body are bound? What sorts of bindings are holding them down? What are your bindings made of? You are starting to realize how the offence you have suffered is tying you down. Gradually, you become aware that it really is you over there, bound to that chair. You go inside yourself so that you are now one with the person who is tied up.

Then you realize that you are not alone in the room; you sense the presence of a powerful being. You recognize Jesus (or any other spiritual being who is important to you). He asks you: "Do you want me to help you release yourself?" Surprised by his offer, you ask: "Do I really want to be released?" "What shall I become without my chains?" "Will I be able to tolerate this new state of freedom?" "What advantages are there to me if I stay a prisoner?" Take a few moments to discuss these important questions.

If you want to be released, tell Jesus. Tell him about what's holding you down and preventing you from forgiving your offender. As you gradually identify each of the obstacles to forgiveness, watch Jesus as he slowly undoes your bindings.

Each time some part of your body is released, stop to savour the relief your new-found freedom offers. As the bindings are gradually untied, let harmony, serenity and peace overtake your whole being.

In this state of grace, where you feel empowered by divine love, watch the person who offended you come towards you. Can you begin to recognize that something has changed in you? Look carefully into this person's eyes. Do you feel you can say to him in all honesty: "I forgive you"? If yes, do so. If not, come back within yourself and ask yourself which of your ties are still holding you down. You can resume the dialogue with Jesus to ask him if he could release you from these last few obstacles to forgiveness. Or, you can stop here and resume this guided imagery exercise later, so you can journey farther down the path of forgiveness. The day will come when, to your surprise, forgiveness will flow like a stream from your heart.

If you were able to release all your bindings, ask yourself what you will do with them in the future. They may serve as symbols, reminding you of the valuable lessons you have just drawn from this experience.

How will you now go about celebrating your new freedom?

When you feel you are ready, get up and leave the room. Open the oak door and walk up the seven stairs to the light of day. Little by little, reconnect with the outside world. Become aware of the sounds. Open your eyes. You feel calm, relaxed, fresh and alert.

You might want to share your impressions with someone, or write them in your journal.

Forgive Us Our Trespasses

Lord, forgive us our trespasses,

> Not to the extent of our pitiful act of forgiveness
> Not as we are accustomed to forgiving
> Not as with our mercenary and calculating
> acts of forgiveness

But rather

> To discover your "gentle mercy"
> To experience your "disarming tenderness"
> To learn in our turn to forgive
> To forgive those with whom we share pain
> To not fall into despair and shame
> To renounce the selfish wish to forgive
> To unmask our self-righteousness and indignation
> To be able to forgive ourselves
> So that our acts of forgiveness may become
> reflections of your own

Lord, forgive us our trespasses.

CHAPTER 19

Step Twelve
Decide Whether to End or Renew the Relationship

Mended friendships demand more care than
those which have never been broken.

— LA ROCHEFOUCAULD

Do you want
to pursue this
relationship in
order to strengthen
it or would it be
better to end it?

Congratulations! You have reached the last step in your long journey towards forgiveness. Now that you have forgiven your offender, all that is left is to decide what to do with the relationship that still binds the two of you. Do you want to pursue this relationship in order to strengthen it or would it be better to end it?

DON'T CONFUSE FORGIVENESS
AND RECONCILIATION

In some writings, forgiveness is synonymous with reconciliation. Hence, many people are afraid to forgive their offenders because they think they must then reconcile with them and once again risk suffering the same abuse. This was the case with my colleague, a psychologist whose friend had betrayed her confidence. She refused to forgive him for she thought she would then have to trust him again and leave herself vulnerable to his indiscretion. I recently noticed the same fear in a person who was also confusing the act of forgiving with that of reconciling. Here is what happened: a woman fell in love with her Protestant pastor. He too became enamoured of her and responded to her advances, not without some fear for his reputation, for he was married and had children. Certain of this man's love, she left her home to live alone in an apartment. She gave her husband the excuse that she wanted to find herself and reflect on the direction of her life. She really

If reconciliation must be the standard for testing the authenticity of forgiveness, we can understand why so many people refuse to forgive.

wanted to be able to enjoy more intimacy with her lover, who was planning to leave his wife and move in with her. But the pastor's wife found out about the affair and convinced her husband to seek marriage counselling. Finally, she managed to dissuade him from moving in with his mistress.

Our heroine found herself all alone in her apartment and, after giving it some careful thought, decided to return to her home. But her husband, still in shock from her abandonment, demanded formal promises of faithfulness as the essential conditions of forgiveness and any possibility of her returning home. She refused. This was where they stood when they came to me. After a few sessions, I managed to make the husband understand that he could not attach conditions to forgiveness – it had to be given fully and freely. But once he had granted his forgiveness, he could then negotiate the conditions of his wife's homecoming. He too had confused forgiveness and reconciliation.

This confusion is found not only among ordinary people but also among specialists on the subject of forgiveness. Some spiritual masters and theologians make statements such as: "The ultimate goal of forgiveness is reconciliation"; "Forgiveness and reconciliation are inseparable realities"; "Forgiveness is incomplete without reconciliation." It would appear that, for many of them, forgiveness would be akin to forgetting everything, to pretending that nothing had happened and to resuming the relationship as it was before the offence. This way of seeing things falls more into the realm of magical thought than healthy human psychology. If reconciliation must be the standard for testing the authenticity of forgiveness, we can understand why so many people refuse to forgive. They feel as if they are pretending to forgive and, hence, betraying themselves.

After a serious offence, it is impossible to resume the former relationship, for the simple reason that it no longer exists and cannot exist again.

It is evident that the normal and desirable outcome of forgiveness remains reconciliation. This is especially so for people bound by very close ties: spouses, parents, children, friends, neighbours and colleagues. But even if reconciliation is possible, we should not imagine that it implies that everything will go back to the way it was before the offence. After a serious offence, it is impossible to resume the former relationship, for the simple reason that it no longer exists and cannot exist again. At most, we can think of strengthening it or giving it some other form.

FORGIVING AND ENDING A RELATIONSHIP

Reconciliation with the offender is often impossible. Take, for instance, those cases where the offender is unknown, dead or missing, or where the offender is unrepentant or a habitual and irresponsible offender. Should we conclude that forgiveness is then impossible? Not at all. Forgiveness is above all a state of the heart. This is why it is not only possible, but even necessary, to grant it to recover inner peace and freedom, whether or not the offender is available or approachable.

In situations where the person forgiving cannot directly express forgiveness, they can still do so through symbolic actions such as writing a letter but not mailing it, surrounding themselves with something that symbolizes this forgiveness, or making a gesture of reconciliation towards a substitute person or group who in some way represents the offender. This is what happened in a parish whose priest had sexually abused a number of people. The bishop sent a special envoy to help the community move through the process of healing. He held a reconciliation service during which he asked parishioners to look on him as their guilty priest, and to come and shake his hand as a sign of forgiveness. In itself this exercise was most appropriate under the circumstances. Unfortunately, it was premature since the envoy did not allow parishioners time to begin healing their pain and moving through it to their journey of forgiveness.

There are also situations where efforts at reconciliation, as generous as they may be, may prove to be imprudent or even dangerous. This would be the case where violent people, confirmed psychopaths or unscrupulous manipulators are concerned. I do not believe that, in the name of some full-scale forgiveness that would include reconciliation, we have to push heroism to the point where we leave ourselves open to new problems. True forgiveness requires nothing of the sort. As a measure of caution, people could remove themselves from these circumstances, even as they forgive their offender.

Even if forgiveness does not lead to reconciliation, it is nonetheless beneficial in more ways than one to those who forgive. First, the victims will be reconciled with themselves; then, they will no longer feel overwhelmed by resentment and the desire for revenge; they will manage to no longer judge their offenders but to understand them; deep in their hearts, they will be able to wish them all the happiness in the world; they will discover the positive side of the painful situation and, no doubt, they will be able to hope that the benevolence they show towards their offenders might change their heart.

But that is not all. Often an offence committed by one who is close to us makes us aware of our unhealthy dependence on that person. The breakdown of the relationship, as painful as it may be, offers those who have been hurt an ideal opportunity to integrate their past following the loss of a loved one. Re-membering the past means reclaiming all the

The responsibility for change lies not only with the offender but also with the victim.

idealization that we have projected onto this person. In other words, it allows us to reclaim all the love, energy, ideals – all our psychological and spiritual investments – in the loved one. You will find a description of a ritual of re-membering at the end of this chapter.

THE OFFENDER CAN GROW THROUGH THE PROCESS OF RECONCILIATION

Let us now examine the changes that can be made in the victim–offender relationship. First, note that, contrary to what some authors would have you believe (Smedes, 1984), the responsibility for change lies not only with the offender but also with the victim, who must learn to never again put themselves in a situation where they could be victimized. To build the new relationship, both offender and victim must feel that they are involved.

First, offenders will have to recognize their share of responsibility in the problem. They will have to show that they are prepared to hear out the victim and thus to put themselves in the victim's shoes. This will help the offender better gauge the extent and the depth of the pain. Even if the offender cannot eliminate the victim's suffering, the offender can at least listen to the victim. To the fullest extent possible, offenders must repair their wrongs and injustices – damaged material goods, smeared reputations, betrayals of trust and other issues.

What trustworthy guarantee can the offender offer for the future? Are repentance, commitments, promises enough? Good intentions will never be able to replace concrete changes. Offenders will therefore have to ask themselves if they have learned something new about themselves and their way of

The real changes we see in the offenders' behaviour offer the best guarantees for successful reconciliation.

relating intimately to others. The real changes we see in the offenders' behaviour offer the best guarantees for successful reconciliation. Offenders will have to ask themselves these questions: "How did I come to commit such an offence? What was my real motivation? What past family or cultural history pushed me to commit such a hurtful action? Which behaviours could I learn to change in the future? What help will I get for myself to do this?"

I think that the following case of an unfaithful husband illustrates well what I mean by signs of growth in the repentant offender. One day, a husband tells his wife that he has a young mistress. To lessen the shock of the news, he quickly reassures her that nothing will change in their life of twenty-five years of marriage, and he promises that she will always be his first love. His wife expresses her deep pain and disappointment, and then informs him that he simply cannot remain at home at the same time as he is enjoying his new bachelor life. After just a few months of living with his mistress, the man realizes that he is unable to adjust to the character of his young companion. Remembering all the benefits he enjoyed in his married life, he asks to go back. But his wife will have none of it. She refuses to resume their life together unless he does some intensive psychological work on himself. In particular, she wants him to become aware of the reasons behind the affair. He manages to do this with the help of a competent therapist. He realizes that, over the years of his married life, he had been letting his frustrations build up and had suppressed a lot of anger towards his wife. He discovered that he had used his love affair to punish her. On further reflection, he realized that he had been seeking the company of a younger woman to avoid

Victims must also seek out the truth about themselves.

his fear of getting old and dying. Following all this reflection, he decided to make the necessary changes in his attitudes. Only then did he feel ready to resume married life.

THE VICTIM'S GROWTH THROUGH RECONCILIATION

"Why did I get myself into this mess?" is a very valid question that victims often ask themselves. It reminds us that the offender alone does not carry the blame for the painful event. Victims must also seek out the truth about themselves and take advantage of their unfortunate experience to examine some of their attitudes and ways of engaging in intimate relationships.

In the eighth step, I asked you to draw some helpful lessons from this painful offence. One should never forget that the wound of the offence, which upsets habits and destroys parts of our world, is a wonderful opportunity for change.

Now I invite you to answer a few questions. They will help you highlight what you have gained and list what you still have to learn in the area of human relationships.

- What have I learned about myself?
- Am I closer to being my own best friend?
- Have I learned to speak gently to myself?
- Have I replaced "I must" and "I have to" by "I choose to ... "?
- Am I able to refuse to respond to demands from people, especially those I love, in a way that respects my personal limits?

Even a small change in the arena of human relationships will bring about other important changes in you.

- Have I learned to express more spontaneously what I'm feeling? When I want to tell someone what's bothering or hurting me about their behaviour, am I able to share my feelings with sentences starting with "I" (for instance: "I feel irritated when you are late ... ") instead of accusing them with a threatening message that starts with "you" (for instance: "You never think about me when you are late like this ... ")?
- What do I do to overcome my attraction to people who have behavioural problems (for instance: alcoholics, smooth talkers, dependent women, etc.)?
- Have I gained some insight into my unrealistic expectations and demands of others?
- On my journey to forgiveness, to what point have I managed to increase my self-esteem?
- By changing my image of a God of justice, how much closer have I gotten to God as friend and confidant?

I'll admit that this is a demanding program. You don't have to do it all at once. Even if you manage to master only one or two of these new behaviours, you will have reason to be proud of yourself. Even a small change in the arena of human relationships will bring about other important changes in you.

CHANGING RELATIONSHIPS AFTER A SEPARATION

There are situations where it is possible neither to give up a relationship nor to strengthen it. In those cases, we have to think about creating new bonds. I have two particular cases in mind. One is that of people who are separated or divorced and who must maintain cordial parental relations for the sake

Parents often have to define their boundaries.

of their children. The other is that of parents who ask themselves how they have to change their behaviour towards their grown children who have left home. They are aware of the challenge of maintaining distance without breaking their bonds of intimacy.

Let us look first at the case of separated or divorced couples. It is not easy to give up the old habits of married life and transform the spouse-couple into a parent-couple. Joanne, one of my clients, admitted to me how difficult she was finding this. She felt torn by a host of contradictory feelings towards her ex-spouse: resentment and guilt at having been abandoned, jealousy towards his new mate, a tremendous need to continue protecting him. In the midst of this merry-go-round of emotions, she also had to maintain a relationship with him as parents concerned for the well-being of their children. She had to mourn her dream of being a part of a couple so that she could maintain a certain serenity in her role as parent with her former husband. She realized she would never be able to succeed at this unless she managed to forgive him first.

A somewhat similar challenge faces parents who find themselves alone after the departure of their grown children. The experience of their children leaving home, the resulting empty-nest syndrome, and the need to rebuild their life as a couple after many years of parenting, may be difficult. The couple must at all costs protect their new intimacy against periodic invasions by the children. These children never think twice about showing up at their parents' home whenever they feel like it, with friends in tow, to raid the refrigerator or take over the television or the swimming pool. Faced with such an invasion, parents often have to define their boundaries. They

Forgiveness alone does not solve all relationship difficulties.

must therefore remind their children that they left of their own free will and that they will henceforth have to behave as guests. One can imagine the courage shown by parents who have to cut the umbilical cord one more time to establish a new relationship with their grown-up children.

In conclusion, I want to stress once again something we had already suspected: forgiveness alone does not solve all relationship difficulties, since it lacks the magical effects we often attribute to it. Furthermore, once granted, it does not guarantee that the offender will not repeat the offence. Still, the important question to ask yourself is: "Has forgiveness had its beneficial impact on me?" In other words: "Have I been transformed by the experience of the offence and of forgiveness?" Another no less important question is this one: "Has my offender learned something through this whole experience?" If you can answer "yes" to both of these questions, congratulate yourself on the happy outcome of your journey of forgiveness.

Exercise

THE RITUAL OF RE-MEMBERING

The ritual of re-membering is an excellent way of growing following a separation. It is especially effective in those cases where you idealized the person you loved passionately. This means that you have projected onto them that which is undeveloped and unconscious in you. This is one of the outcomes of being in love. It moves you out of yourself to live in the other. If, after forgiveness, you need to end the relationship, all will not be lost. You will still have an opportunity to recover the object of your idealizations and to use it for your own growth. Thus, you can end the relationship without weakening or fooling yourself. This is the objective of the ritual of re-membering that I am about to describe for you.

As with all rituals, that of re-membering will be all the more effective if you arrange for the presence of a leader or celebrant and witnesses who will support you on your journey.

At least two weeks before the ceremony, the leader helps you remember the qualities you were attracted to in the person you love. Four or six such qualities will do. Then, the leader asks you to find some objects that symbolize these same qualities.

It is important for the ceremony to take place in a setting that touches all the senses, so use incense, candles, flowers, colourful tablecloths, etc.

On the day of the ceremony, you and the leader stand in front of a table where you have laid out the objects symbolizing the qualities you named. The witnesses stand in a semi-circle in front of the table.

After explaining the meaning of the ceremony, the celebrant invites you to introduce the loved one through the qualities represented by the symbols. Once you have finished the introduction, you sit back down next to the celebrant. All of the participants observe a few minutes of meditative silence.

The leader then invites you to pick out the object symbolizing the first quality and invites you to repeat the following formula of re-membering: "_____ (name of the loved one), because we are now separated, I am retrieving _____ (the desired quality such as, for instance, the sense of humour) that I attributed to you, some _____ (length of the relationship) ago, and that you enriched with your own _____ (example: sense of humour)."

You take your place, clutching the symbol to your heart. The leader helps you integrate the new quality into your person by telling you: "Feel the presence of this new quality as a part of yourself, hear it speak in you, see it inside yourself." He or she continues to encourage you to make the quality you had projected onto your beloved part of yourself. For a few minutes, the leader lets the re-membering proceed, and then invites you to get the next object symbolizing another quality, and takes you through the same steps with this symbol. The leader repeats the same process for each of the remaining qualities.

At the end, you stand in the middle of the group, surrounded by the symbols. The leader of the ritual declares that your mourning is over, the participants congratulate you and finish the ceremony with a party.

This is the outline of the ritual of re-membering. Nothing prevents you from adding other elements to enhance its intensity and beauty.

CHAPTER 20

Celebrating Forgiveness

That which is not celebrated tends to wane and
fade away without a trace.

— ANONYMOUS

Just as the mountain climber who has reached the summit of the mountain takes time to look at the view and contemplate the course of the ascent, so you are invited to stop at the top of your climb and look back over the road you have covered.

From the outset, you have tried to avoid the dead end of resentment and revenge. Furthermore, because you did not want to let the offender hassle you further, you did everything you could to make that person stop any unjust or offensive action directed at you.

You have not been afraid to delve deep within yourself and touch the profound shame caused by wounds from childhood or adulthood. This allowed you to embark on your journey of healing.

You resisted closing yourself off and suffering alone. You shared the weight of your suffering with someone who lent you a sympathetic ear. This helped you see clearly to the very depths of your being.

You managed to define the extent of your loss well enough to name it and mourn it.

You faced your anger and your desire for vengeance and befriended them. You saw in them the positive energies that were ready to preserve your threatened personal integrity.

Little by little, you learned to nurture your self-esteem in preparation for forgiving yourself.

You tried to understand your offender. You stopped seeing him or her in a bad light so you could see yourself in a better light.

You reflected on the positive meaning you were going to give the wound inflicted by the offence.

You let the love shown you by others through their acts of forgiveness soften your heart, and you nourished yourself with this incomparable sensation of feeling forgiven and worthy of forgiveness.

You learned to detach yourself even from your act of forgiveness. You renounced the need to feel as if you were solely responsible for forgiveness, and thus avoided using it to glorify yourself.

You questioned your image of a God of justice to let yourself discover the God of tenderness and mercy, a necessary source of inspiration and strength for forgiveness.

Finally, you decided to examine your future relationship with your offender. You decided either to let them leave, while wishing them all the happiness in the world, or you formed a new covenant with them.

Once you have completed this review of your journey of forgiveness, you should be proud of yourself.

Congratulate yourself!

Celebrate yourself!

You have grown in humanness and holiness!

Here we are, at the end of a long journey. I hope I will not have to face the comment that an older nun made to a young priest who had just finished preaching a retreat on mysticism: "Father, I am surprised to see you juggling such hot coals without burning yourself." Writing on forgiveness carries many similar risks, for it is a hazardous journey. As I wrote, I felt – and still feel – vulnerable in the face of the extent, the complexity and the depth of the topic. Speaking about forgiveness is more than talking about love; it is speaking about a particular type of love, a love that is prepared to go beyond itself to strive to create a new relational universe.

My friend's question that I shared with you in the Foreword still plagues me: "What is it that you are trying to learn about yourself in writing a book about forgiveness?" Certainly, I have discovered my own weaknesses when faced with my own need to forgive. In addition to the new knowledge my research offered me, I have the feeling that I better understand the importance and benefits of forgiveness in my own life, as much from the physical as from the psychological and spiritual points of view. In particular, I ask myself whether I should attribute a noticeable drop in my blood pressure to my reflections on forgiveness. Who knows?

As for the objectives I had set for myself with this book, I am inclined to ask myself whether they have been attained. In other words, have I managed to demystify and unmask the false conceptions about forgiveness? Have I marked out the path to forgiveness clearly enough to allow someone else to set out on it with confidence and without emptying it of its mystery? Have I done it so that the person who is forgiving doesn't get lost in a labyrinth that, attractive as it may seem, leads nowhere? Finally, am I right in believing that the process of forgiveness that I propose, with its twelve reference points, will provide the inner liberation and peace of mind to those who need it? Only you, my readers, can tell me.

APPENDIX

A brief description of other authors' ideas about
the process of forgiveness and its steps

There is some value to comparing the various ways of
conceiving of the dynamics of forgiveness. They vary
according to each author in terms of the number and
nature of steps suggested. In *Putting Forgiveness into Practice* (1982),
Doris Donneley splits the process of forgiveness into five steps:
recognizing the injury, deciding to forgive, becoming aware of
the difficulty of forgiving, forgiving, examining the harmful
effects of the absence of forgiveness. In *Forgiving from the Heart*
(1983), David Norris also recommended five steps: the intention to forgive the trespass, the need to relive the trespass as
accurately as possible, the discovery of the new meaning taken
on by current injury and previous injuries, repairing the broken
relationship, reintegrating the parts of one's being that have
been thrown askew by the current and previous injuries. In *Forgive
and Forget* (1984), Lewis Smedes describes the process of forgiveness in four stages: hurting, hating, healing, reconciling. In
his article "Forgiving: An Essential Element in Effective Living"
(1985), Richard Walters suggests a five-step process of forgiveness: 1) pray to prepare for forgiveness, especially to recognize
the need to forgive, to awaken the desire to forgive, to learn to
master your resentment and find the courage to persevere on
your path of forgiveness; 2) decide to forgive without forgetting;
3) fulfill the act of forgiving; 4) celebrate the forgiveness granted; 5) follow through on your forgiveness: reconcile or end the
relationship. In the popular book *Healing Life's Hurts* (1974), the
brothers Matthew and Dennis Linn borrow from Elisabeth
Kübler-Ross the five steps through which a person who is in
mourning must pass: refusal, anger, bargaining, depression and
acceptance.

"Agresseur, mon frére" in *Prier*, 89 (1987), 5-6.

Arendt, Hannah. *The Human Condition.* Chicago: University of Chicago Press, 1998.

Augsburger, D. *Caring Enough to Forgive: True Forgiveness; Caring Enough to Not Forgive: False Forgiveness.* Ventura, California: Regal Books, 1981.

Bellet, M. L. *Écoute.* Paris: Desclée de Brower, 1989.

Blais, Roger and Laroche, Thérèse. *Le pardon de l'autre dans la guérison intérieure. Théorie et étude de cas.* Ottawa: 1987. Master's thesis directed by Jacques Gagné and presented to the Pastoral Institute of Saint Paul University, Ottawa, in fulfillment of the requirements for a Master's Degree in Pastoral Counselling.

Bradshaw, J. *Healing the Shame that Binds You.* Deerfield Beach, Florida: Health Communications, 1988.

Carmignac, J. *A l'écoute du Notre Père.* Paris, O.E.I.L.: 1984.

——*Recherches sur le Notre Père.* Paris: Éditions Letouzey et Ané, 1969.

Cunningham, B. B. "The Will to Forgive: A Pastoral Theological View of Forgiving," in *Journal of Pastoral Care,* 39, 2 (1985), 141-149.

Davy, M. M. *Un philosophe itinérant.* Gabriel Marcel. Paris: Flammarion, 1959.

Donnely, D. "Forgiveness and Recidivism" in *Pastoral Psychology,* 33, 1 (1984), 15-24.

Putting Forgiveness into Practice. Allen, Texas: Argus Communications, 1982.

Droll, D. M. *Forgiveness: Theory and Research.* Nevada: 1984. Dissertation submitted in partial fulfillment of the requirements for the degree of Doctor of Philosophy in Social Psychology, University of Nevada, 1984.

Duquoc, C. "The Forgiveness of God" (translated by Iain McGonagle), in *Concilium*, 184 (1986), 35-44.

Elizondo, V. "I Forgive but I Do Not Forget," in *Concilium*, 184 (1986), 69-79.

Emerson, J. G. *The Dynamics of Forgiveness.* London: George Allen and Unwin Ltd., 1965.

Enright, R. D. and Joanna North (Eds.). *Exploring Forgiveness.* Madison, WI: The University of Wisconsin Press, 1998.

Fitzgibbons, M. "The Cognitive and Emotive Use of Forgiveness in the Treatment of Anger" in *Psychotherapy*, 23 (1986), 629-633.

Frankl, V. E. *Man's Search for Meaning.* New York: Washington Square Press, 1984.

Gagey, J. "De la miséricorde envers soi-même" in *La vie spirituelle. Difficultés du pardon*, 131 (619, 1977), 41-56.

Gagné, J. *Le pardon, une dimension essentielle des études et de la pratique pastorales*, Colloque internationale en études pastorales. Ottawa: Université Saint-Paul, 1988.

Gouhier, A. *Pour une métaphysique du pardon.* Paris: Épi, 1969.

Guillet, J., and Marty, F. "Pardon" in *Dictionnaire de spiritualité*, tome XII, 1st Part. Paris: Beauchesne, 1984.

Hatzakortzian, S. *Le pardon, une puissance qui libère.* St-Badolph: Éditions Compassion, 1980.

Hope, D. "The Healing Paradox of Forgiveness," in *Psychotherapy*, 24, 2 (1987), 240-244.

Hunter, R. "Forgiveness, Retaliation and Paranoid Reactions" in *Canada Psychiatric Association Journal*, 23 (1978), 167-173.

Jankelevitch, V. *Le pardon*. Paris: Aubier-Montaigne, 1967.

Le pardon. Juifs, Chrétiens, Musulmans, Supplément du Bulletin de Littérature Ecclésiastique, Institut catholique de Toulouse, Chronique I, 1989. Colloquium, January 30-31, 1988.

Linn, D., Linn, M. and Fabricant, S. *Prayer Course for Healing Life's Hurts*. Paulist Press, 1983.

Linn, D., and Linn, M. *Healing Life's Hurts: Healing Memories Through Five Stages of Forgiveness*. Paulist Press, 1987.

Madre, P. *Mystère d'amour et ministère de guérison*. Paris: Pneumathèque, 1982.

Monbourquette, J. *To Love Again: Finding Comfort and Meaning in Times of Grief.* Ottawa: Novalis, 1993.

Morrow, L. Reported by Barry Kalb and Wilton Wynn/Rome, "Cover Story: I Spoke as a Brother": A Pardon from the Pontiff. A Lesson in Forgiveness for a Troubled World, *Time*, 123, January 9 (1984), 22-28.

Norris, D. A. *Forgiving from the Heart: A Biblical and Psychotherapeutic Exploration*. Union Seminary: 1983 [Ann Arbor, University Microfilms International]. Ph.D. dissertation.

Pattison, E. "On Failure to Forgive and Be Forgiven" in *American Journal of Psychotherapy*, 19 (1965), 106-115.

Patton, J. *Is Human Forgiveness Possible?* Nashville, Abingdon Press, 1985.

Perrin, M., editor. *Le pardon.* Paris: Beauchesne, 1987. Papers from a colloquium organized by the Centre d'Histoire et des Idées, Université de Picardie.

Peters, J. "The Function of Forgiveness in Social Relationships," translated by Robert Nowell, in *Concilium*, 184 (1986), 3-11.

Rubio, M. "The Christian Virtue of Forgiveness," translated by G.W.S. Knowles, in *Concilium*, 184 (1986), 80-94.

Soares-Prabhu, G. "As We Forgive: Interhuman Forgiveness in the Teachings of Jesus," in *Concilium*, 184 (1986), 57-66.

Sobrino, J. "Latin America: Place of Sin and Place of Forgiveness," translated by Dinah Livingstone, in *Concilium*, 184 (1986), 45-56.

Studzinski, R. "Remember and Forgive: Psychological Dimensions of Forgiveness," in *Concilium*, 184 (1986), 12-21.

Vanier, J. *Community and Growth: Our Pilgrimage Together.* Toronto: Griffin House, 1979.